*It's an **Underwater** Adam Wallace Colouring Book*

First published in the Year of the Zombie Pirate, 2020, by
Krueger Wallace Press

Email: **wally@adam-wallace-books.com** or visit
www.adam-wallace-books.com or visit
my dad. He has a cool house.

Designer/Typesetter: Adam Wallace

Printed by Lightning Source

Edited by Tex Calahoon

ISBN: 978-0-6482312-9-5

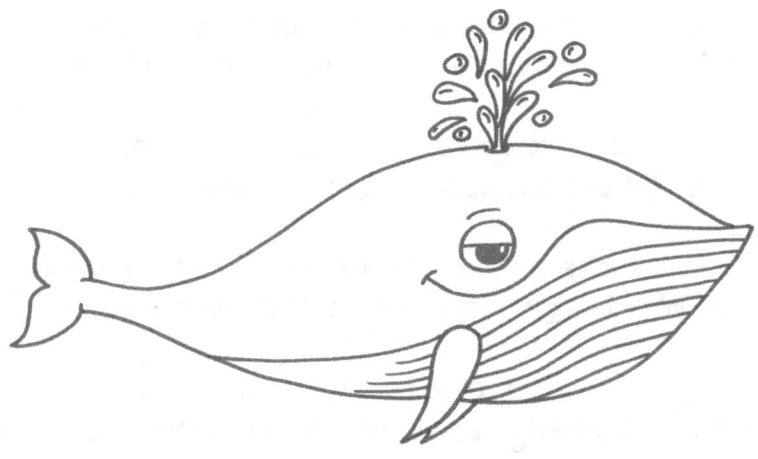

Do not stir-fry this book.
This book is not a box of tissues or a box of kittens.

WELCOME TO THE UNDERWATER ADAM WALLACE COLOURING BOOK

(Adam Wallace isn't underwater ... and you don't colour the pictures underwater, that will ruin the book, and your pencils ... its just the animals you're about to colour in all love the water!)

Grab your colouring implements, whatever you like,
Get ready for your excitement to spike!

It's time to colour in some marine creatures,
Whatever colour you like. Whatever features.

You can use red or green or pink or yellow,
And there's just one rule for you to follow.

Colour these animals **however** you want it done,
If your imagination flies you'll have more fun!

So you get to colouring, I need a rest,
If you send a coloured-in photo to me, that would be **the best!!!**

wally@adam-wallace-books.com is the email to send,
And now it's time for this poem to end!

HAVE FUN!!!

You'll notice that sometimes the eyes on the animals are coloured in, and sometimes they aren't! Sometimes it's to show how *I* colour eyes, sometimes it's so **you** can colour the eyes.

But you may be confused. What bit should you colour in? Well, you have a choice!

So, for example, with this baby crab ...

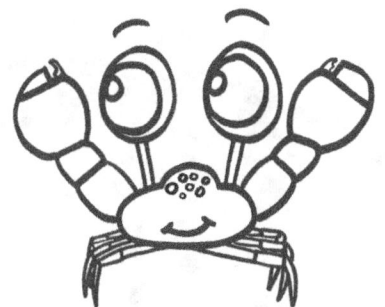

You could colour the small bit ...

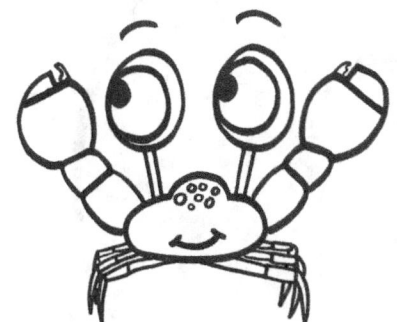

Or the big bit!

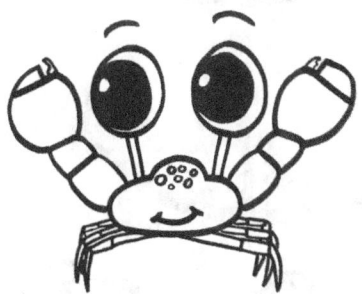

It's up to you. Any circle. Any colour. So now there's only one thing left to do ...

GET COLOURING!!!

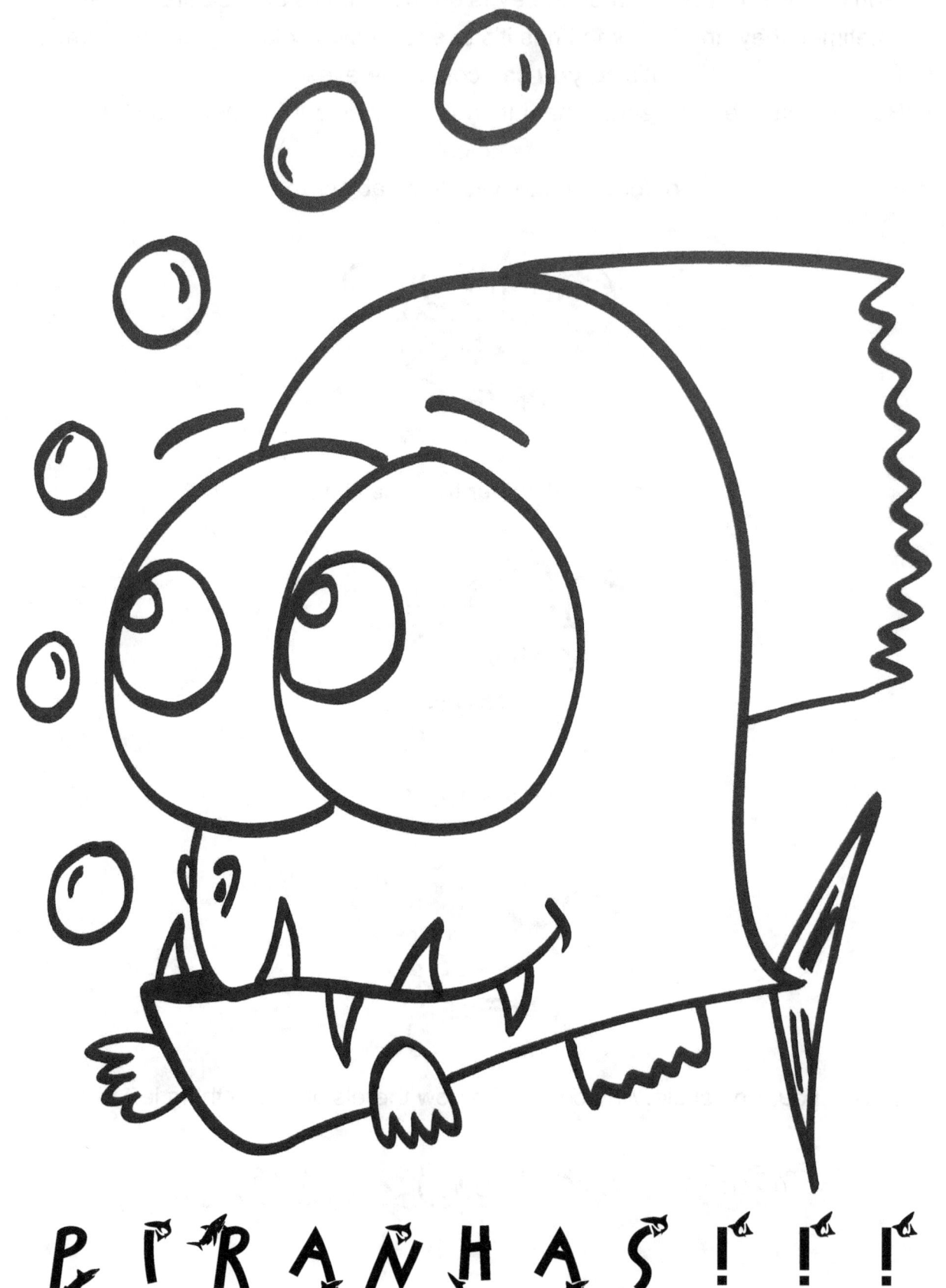

PIRANHAS!!!

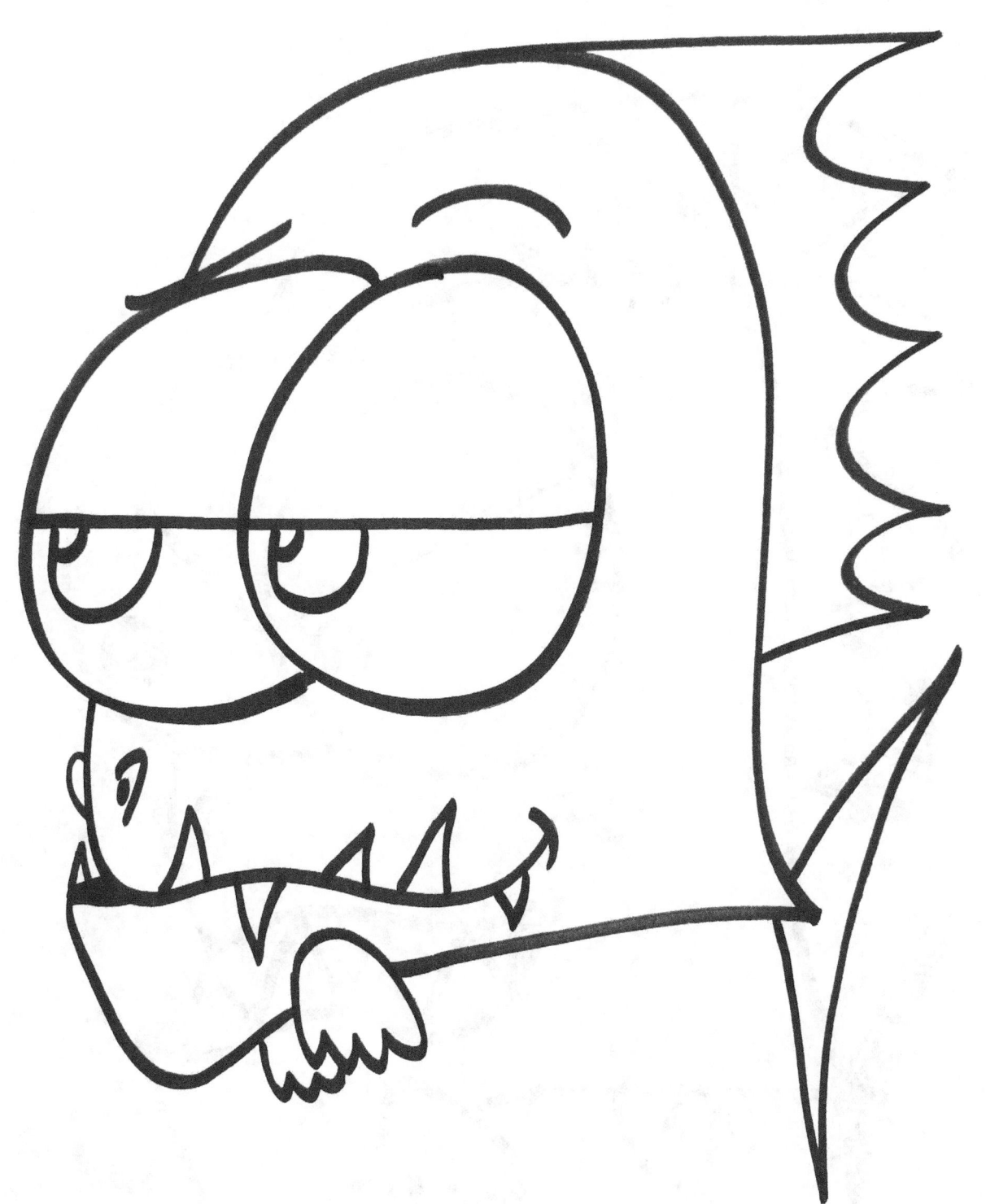

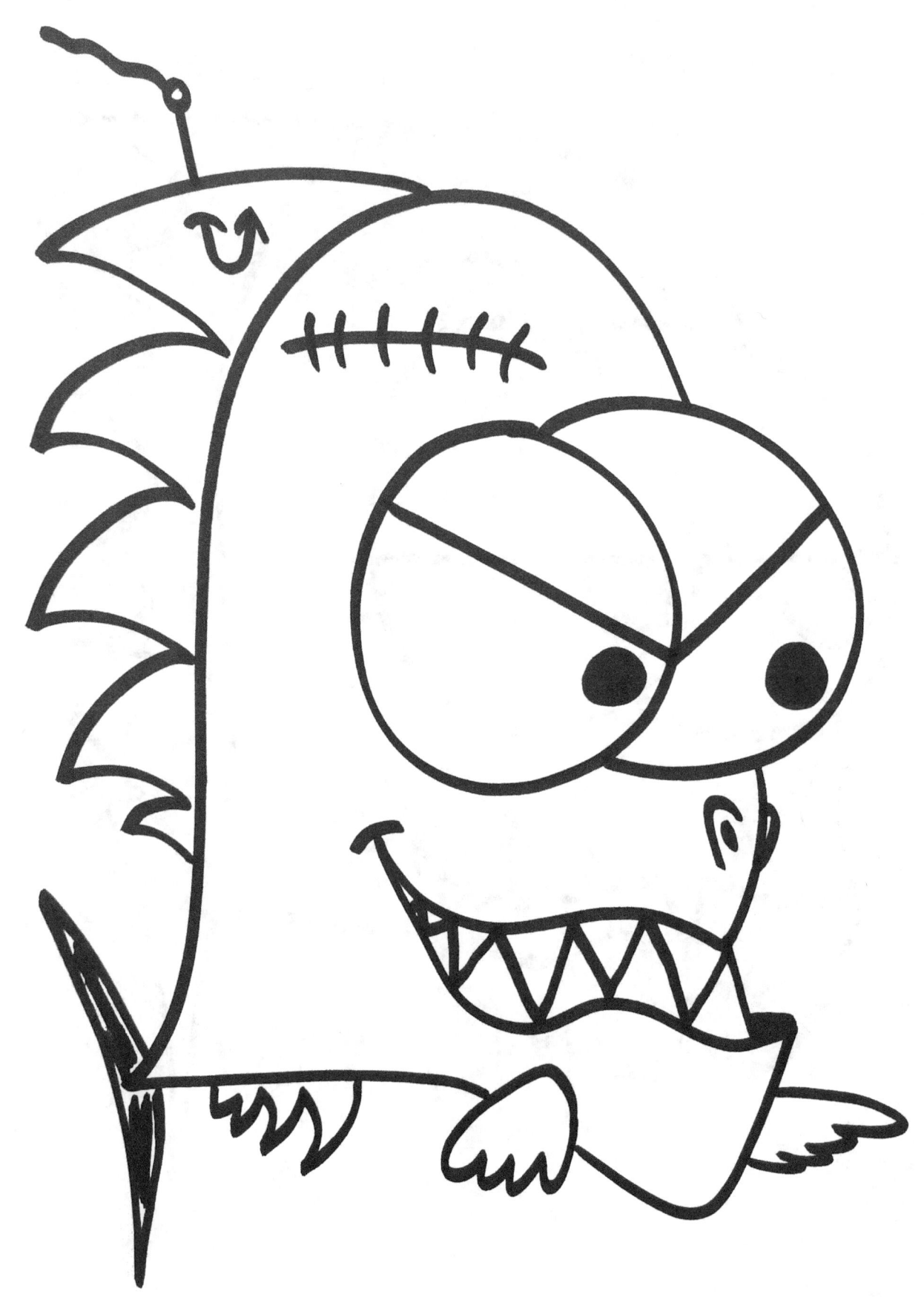

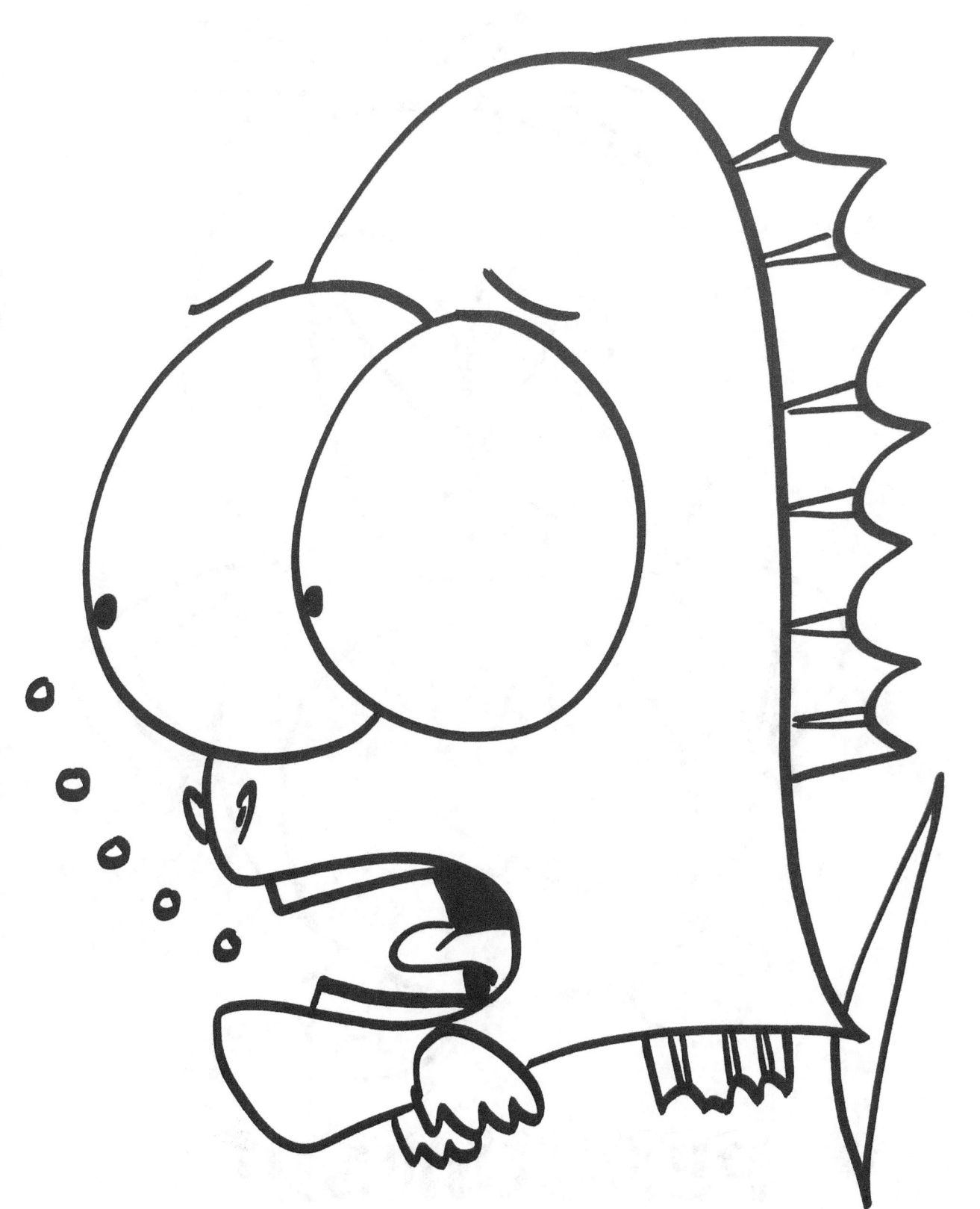

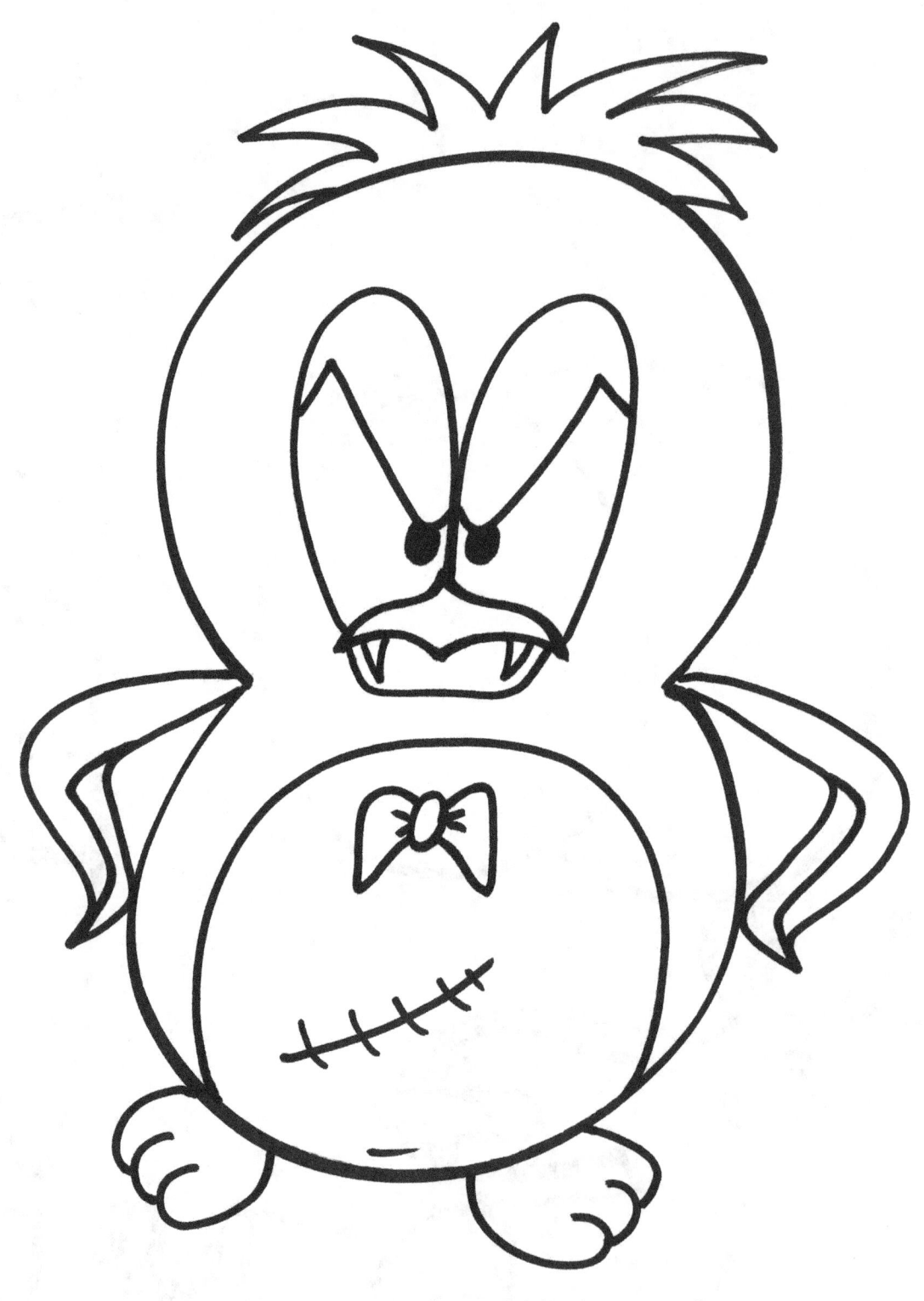

PENGUINS!!!

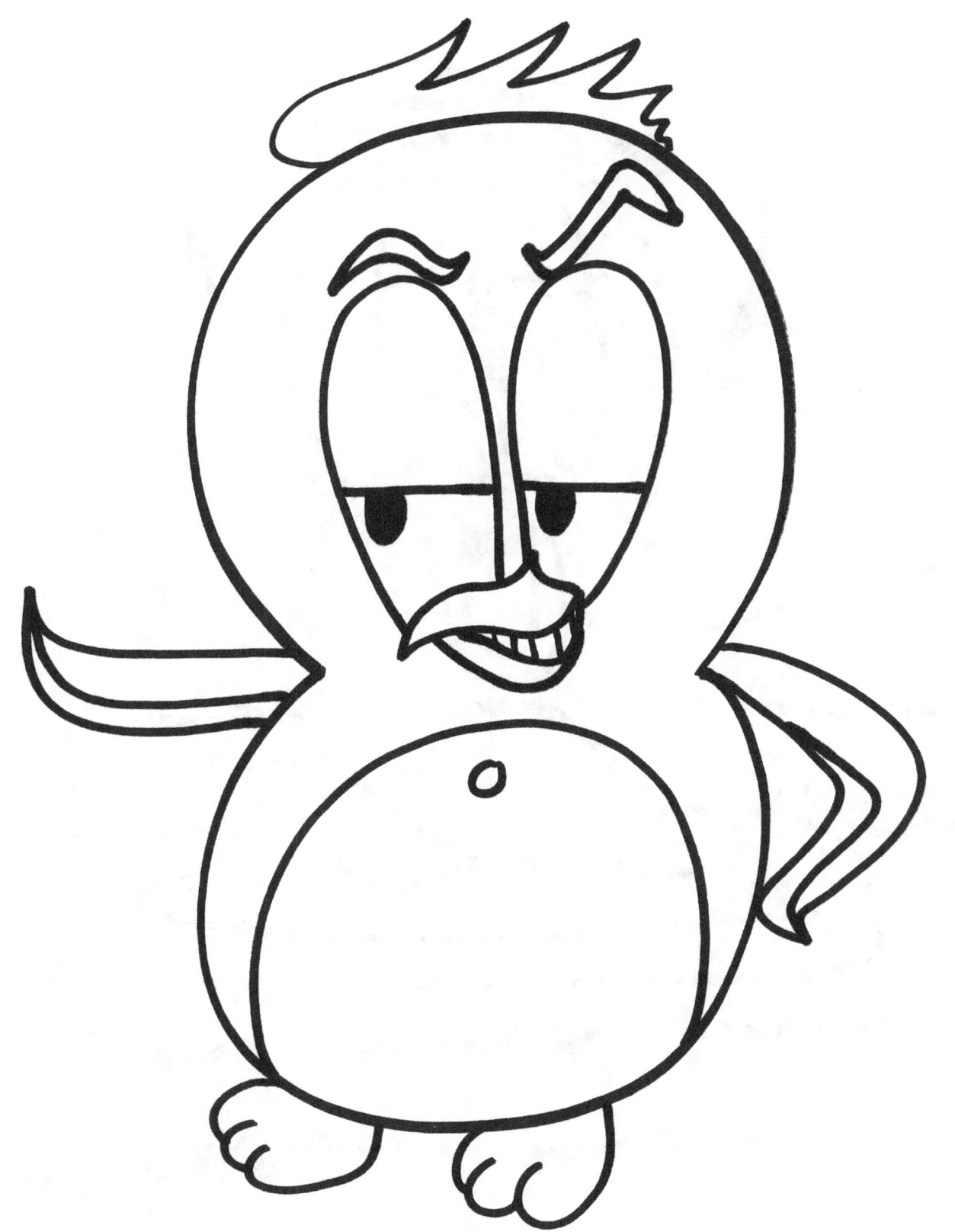

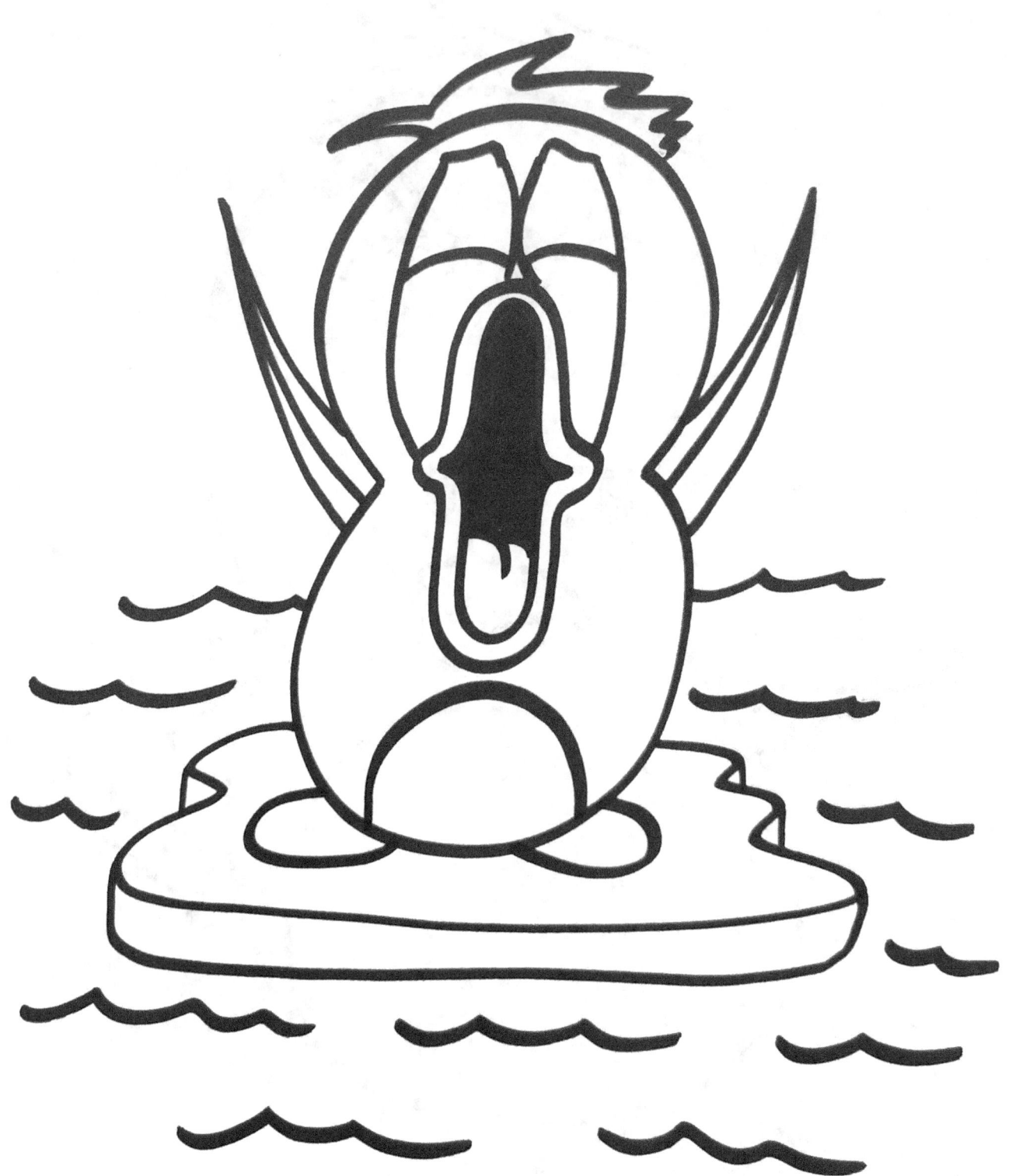

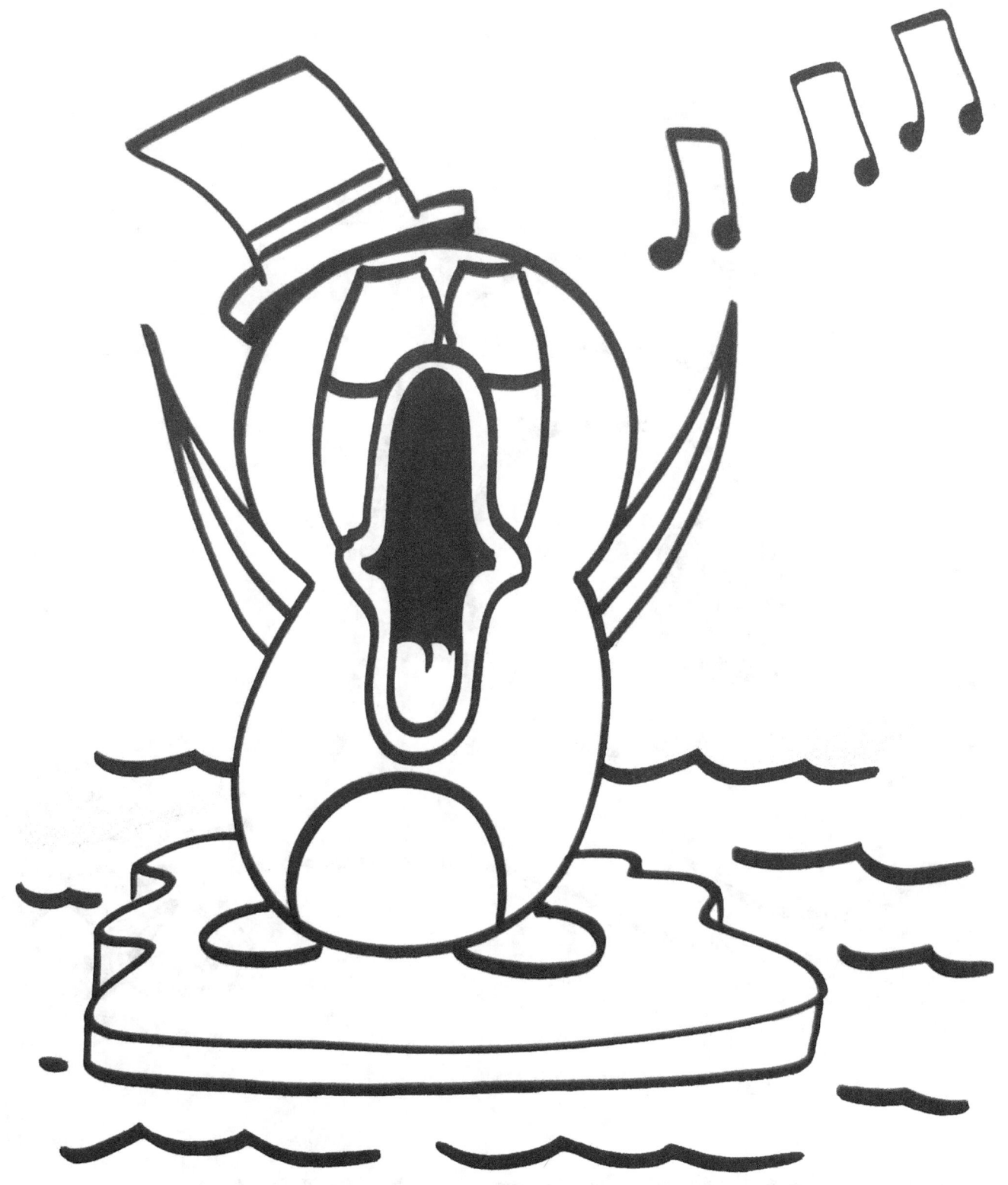

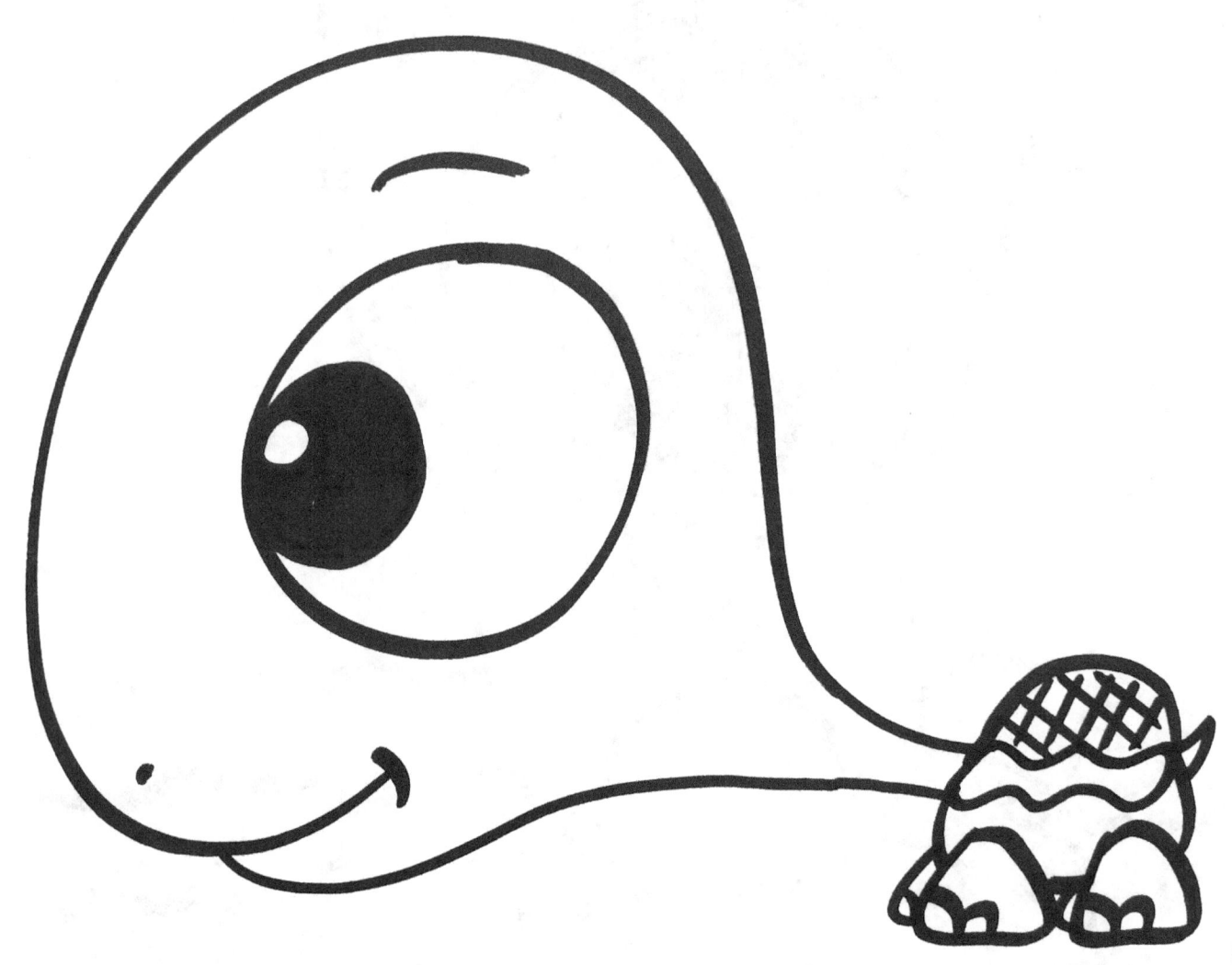

TORTOISES!!!

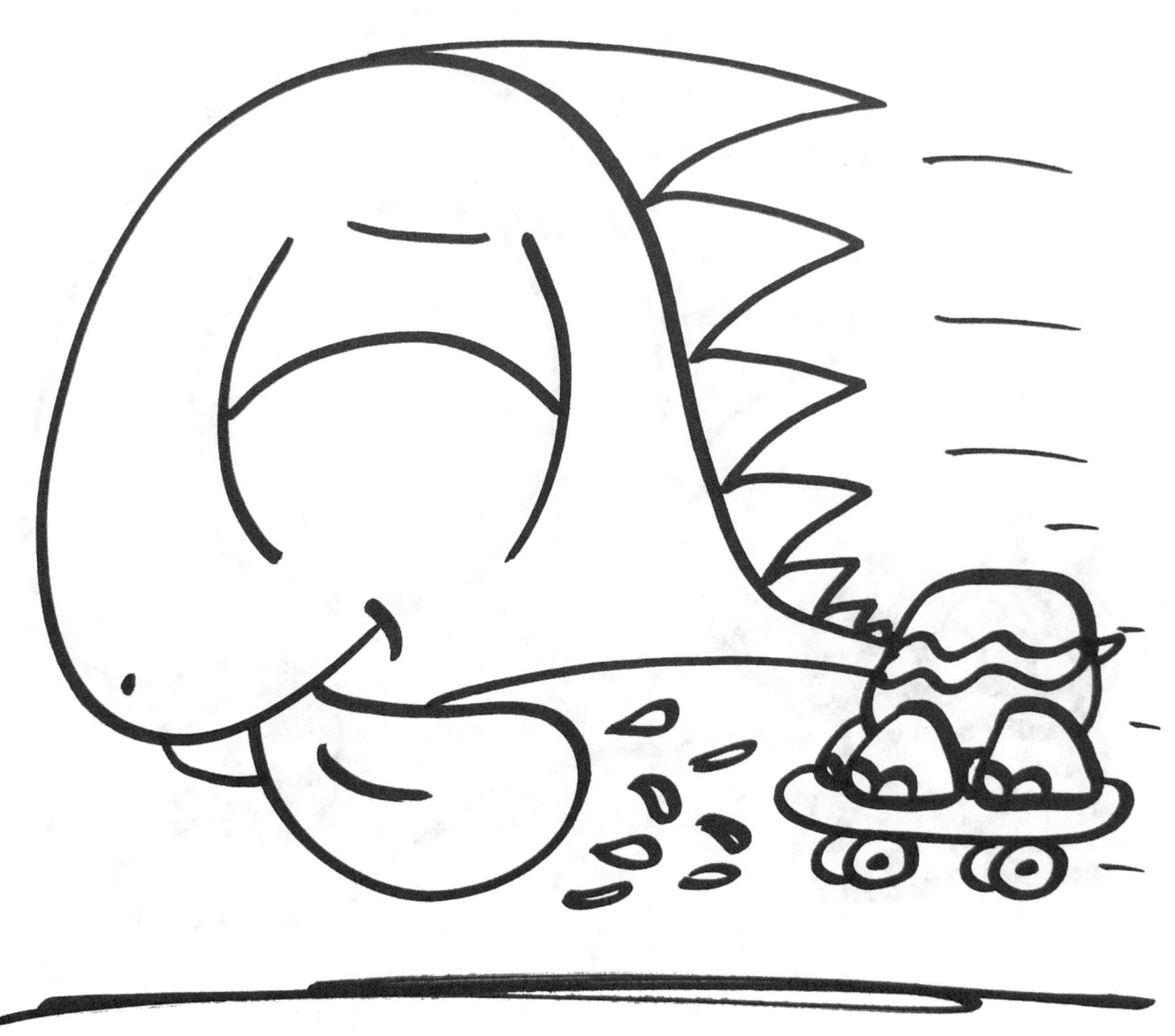

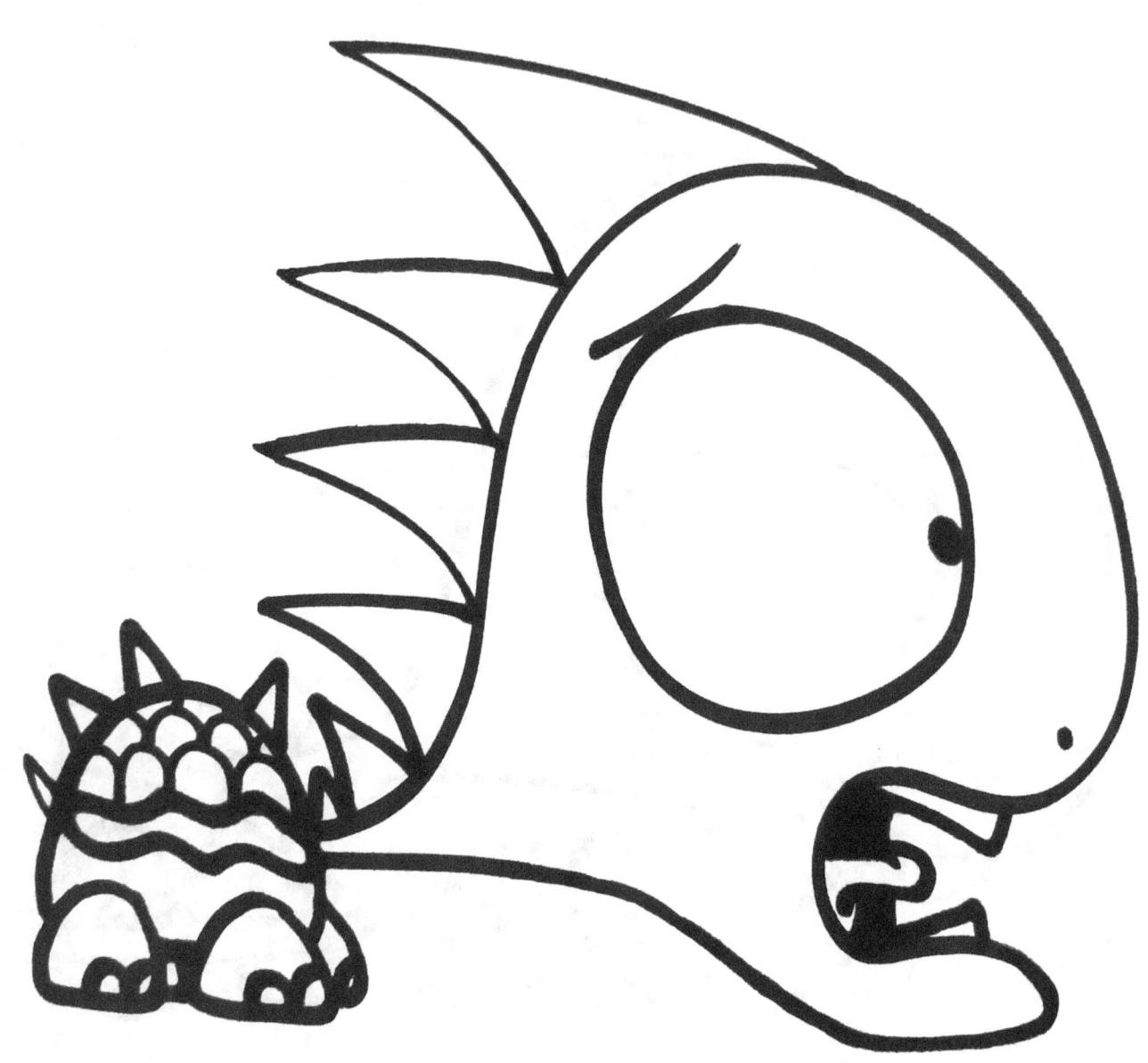

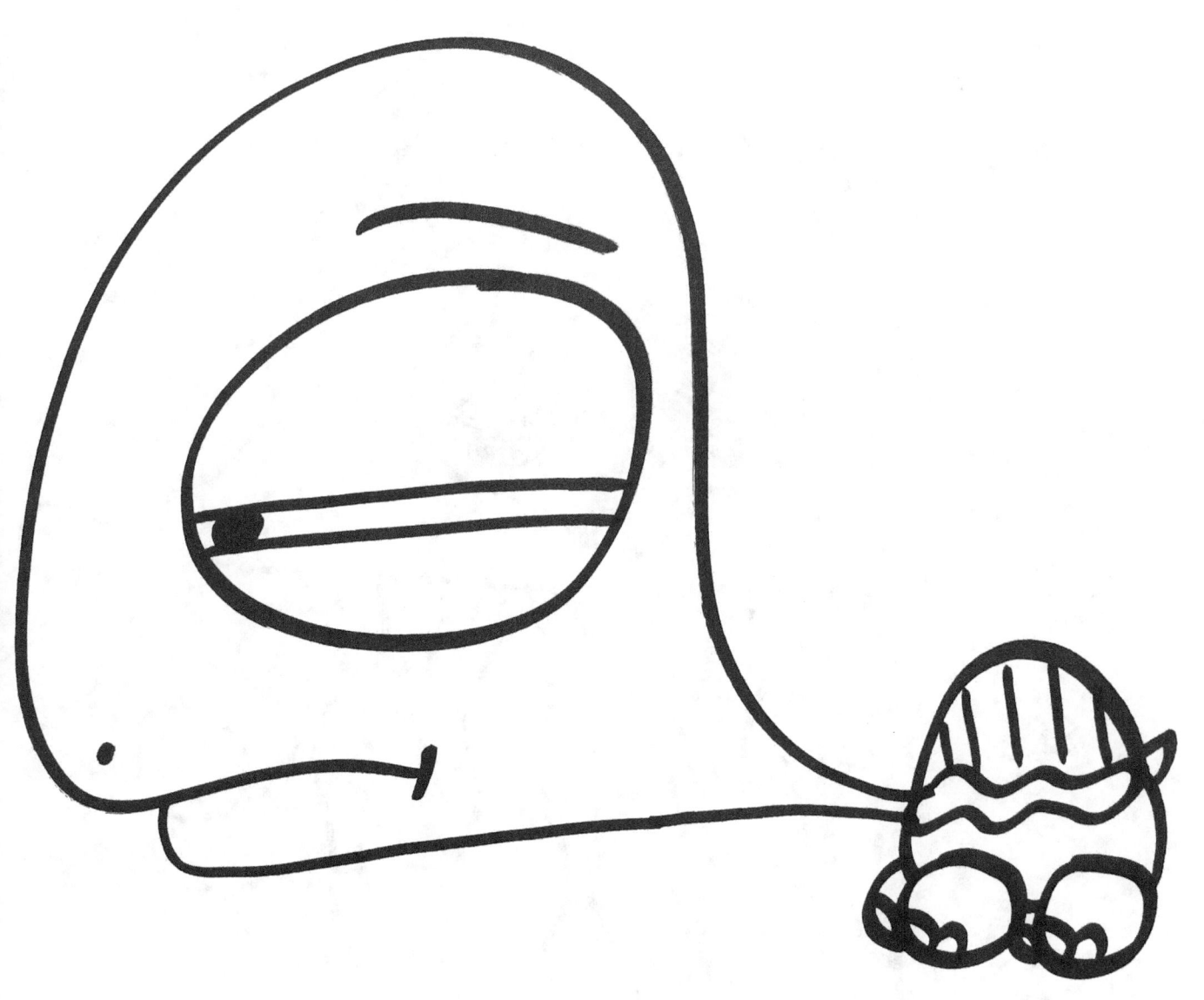

JELLYFISH

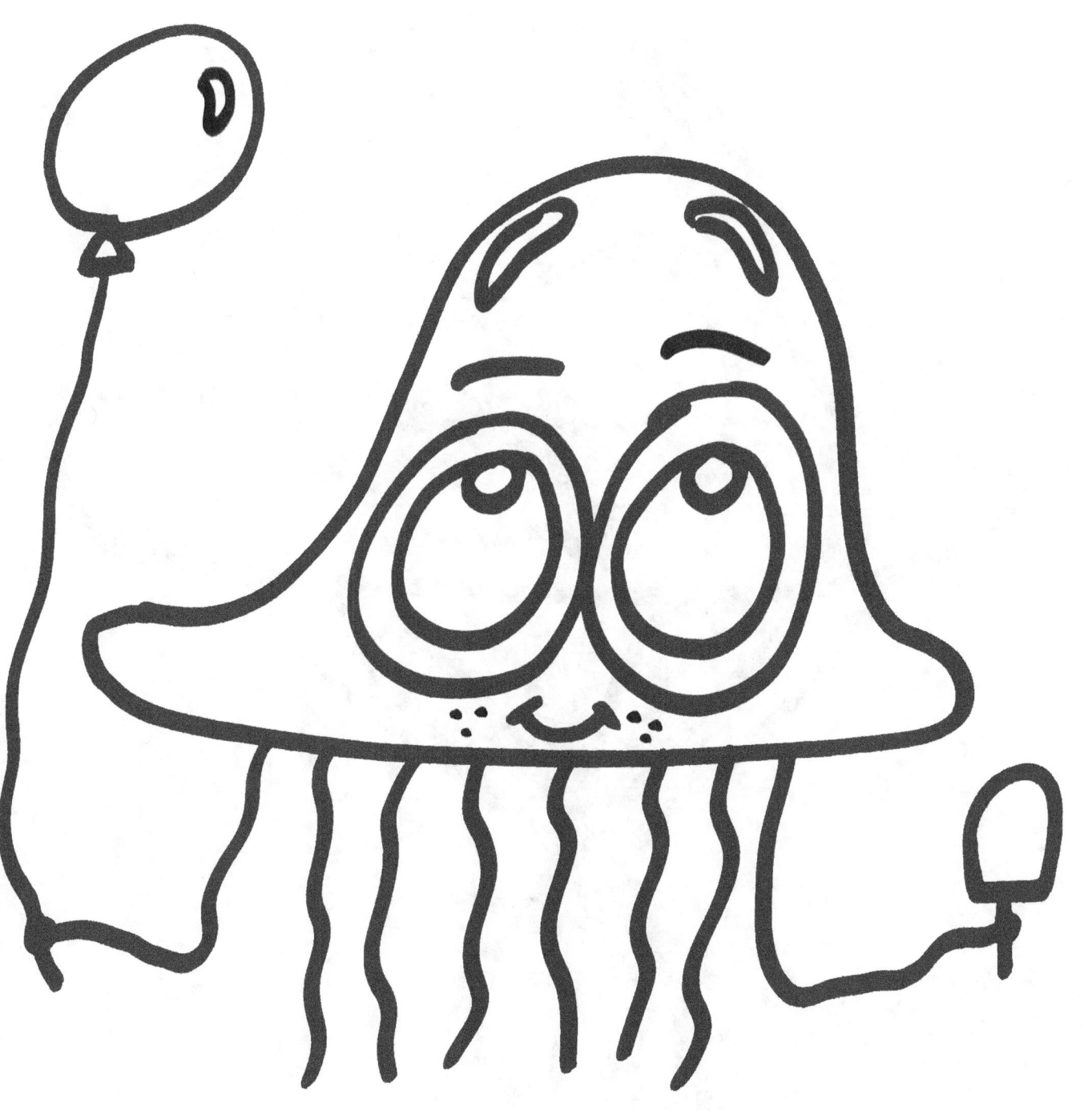

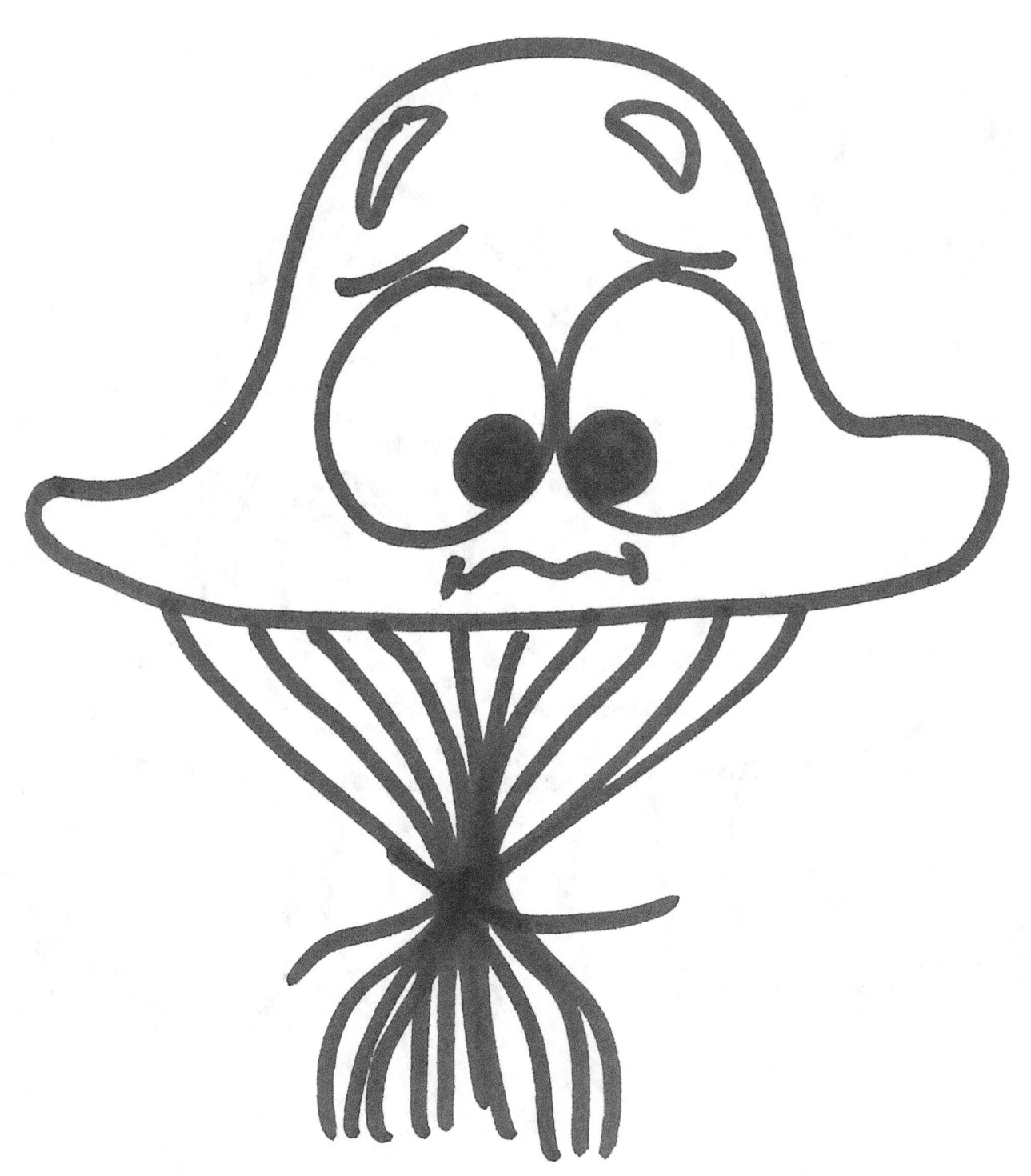

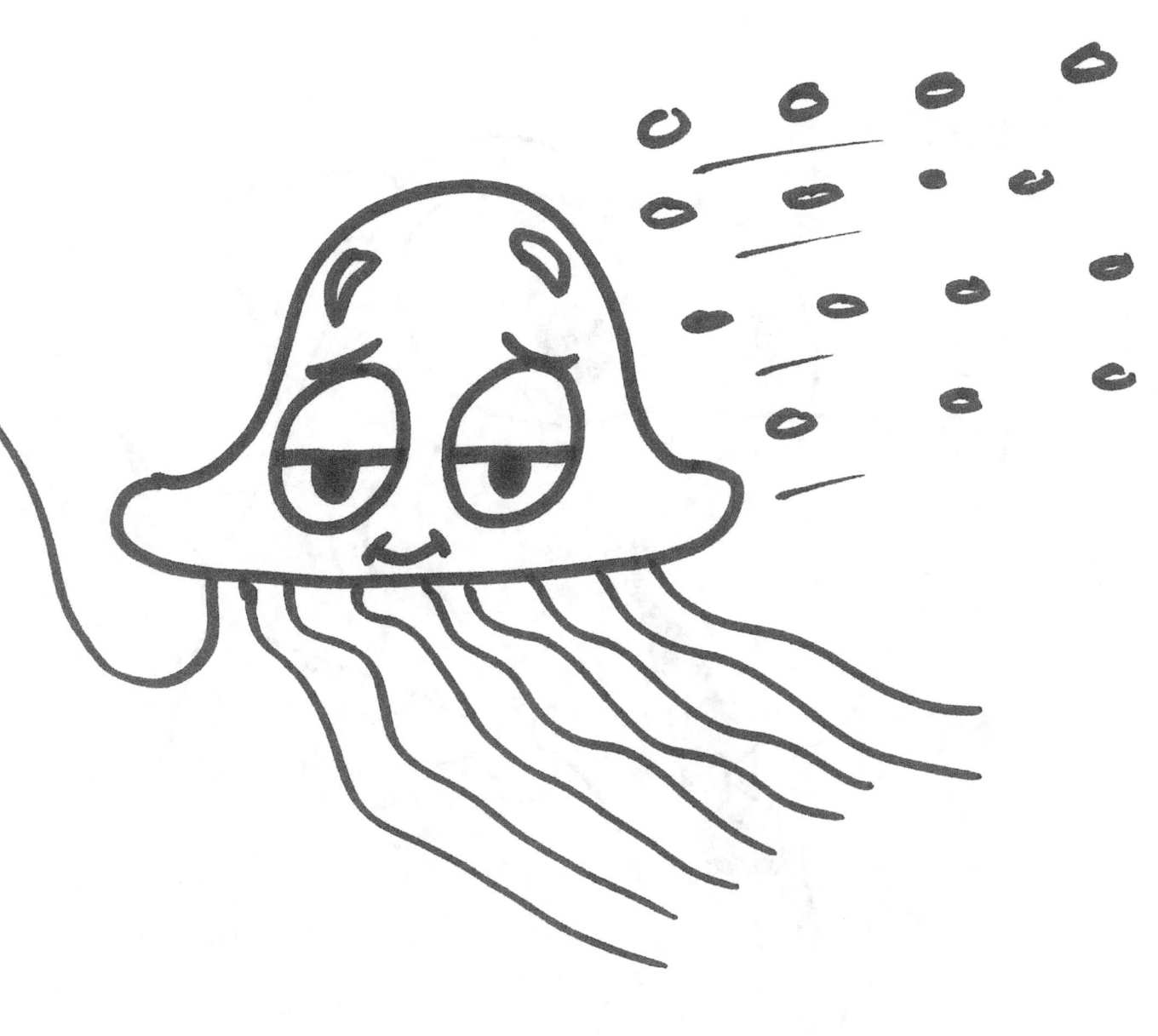

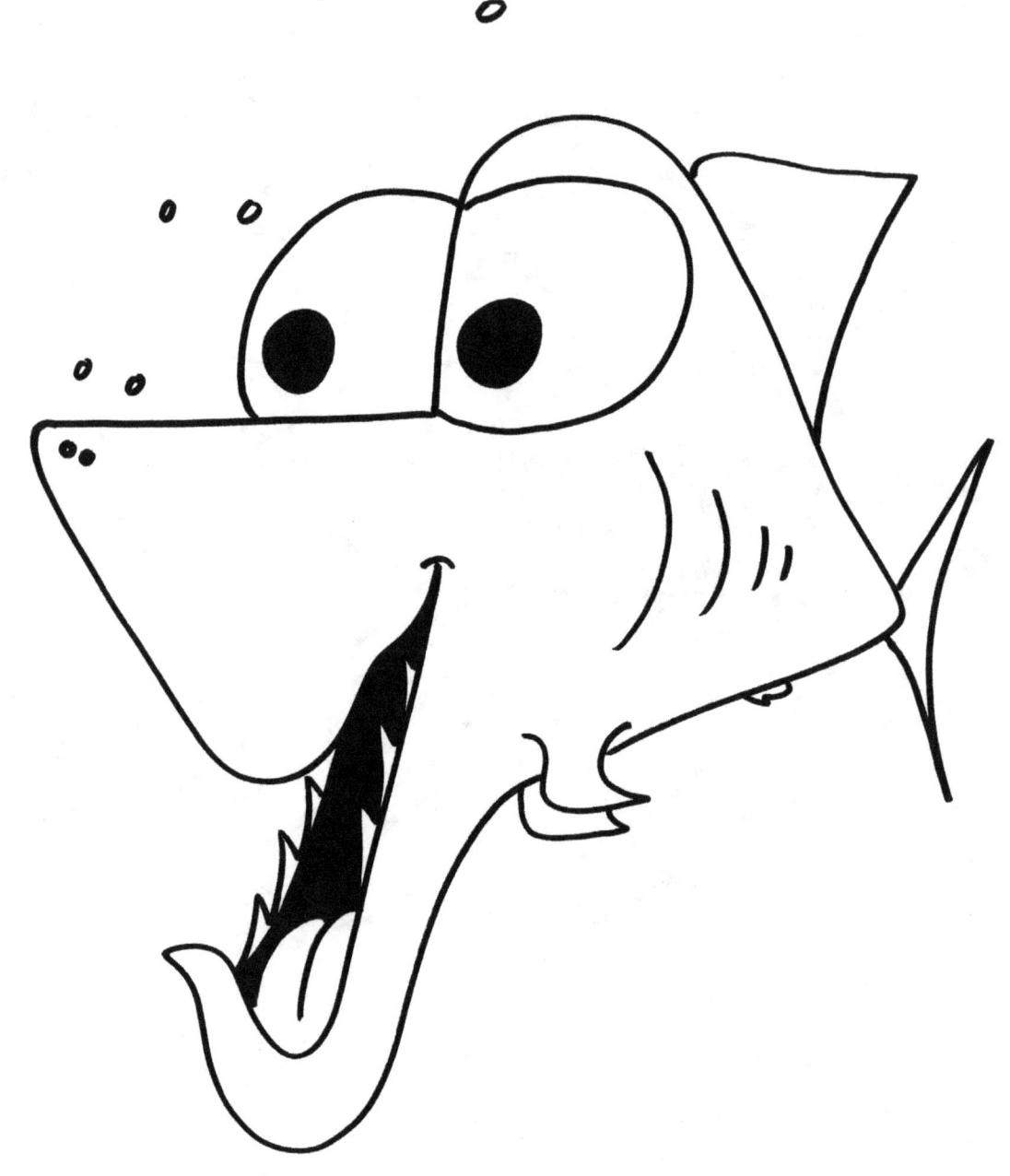

SHARKS!!!!

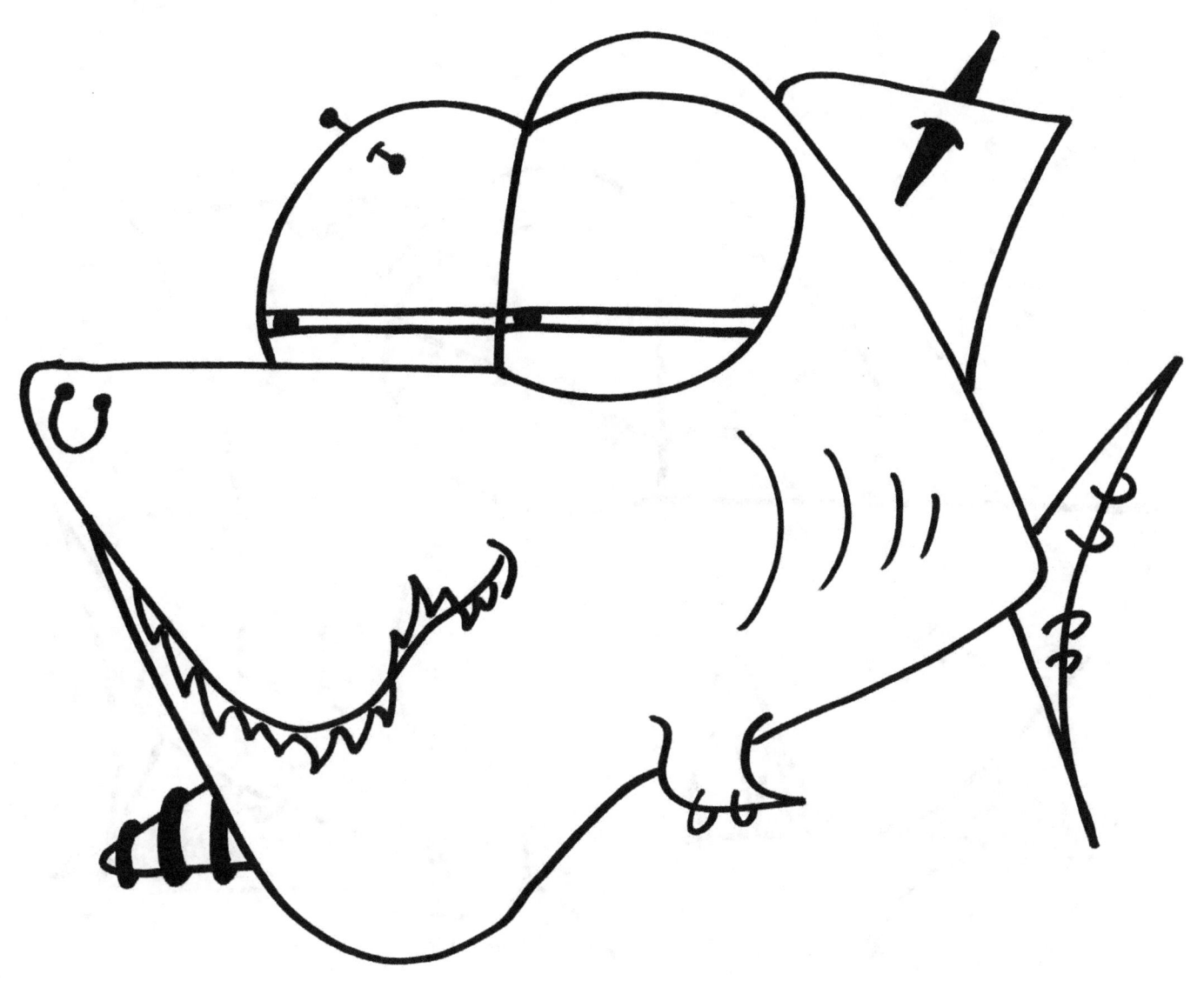

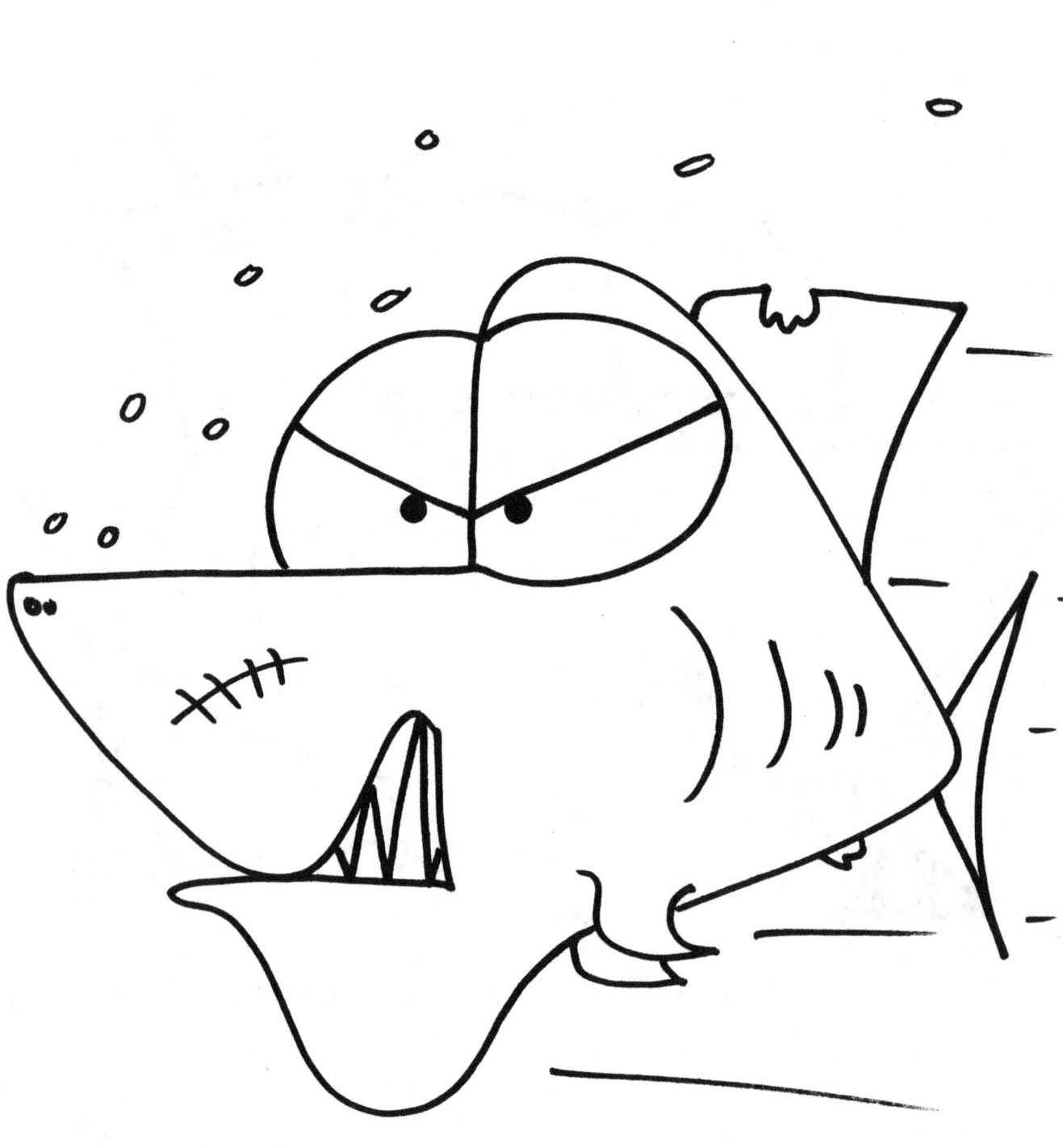

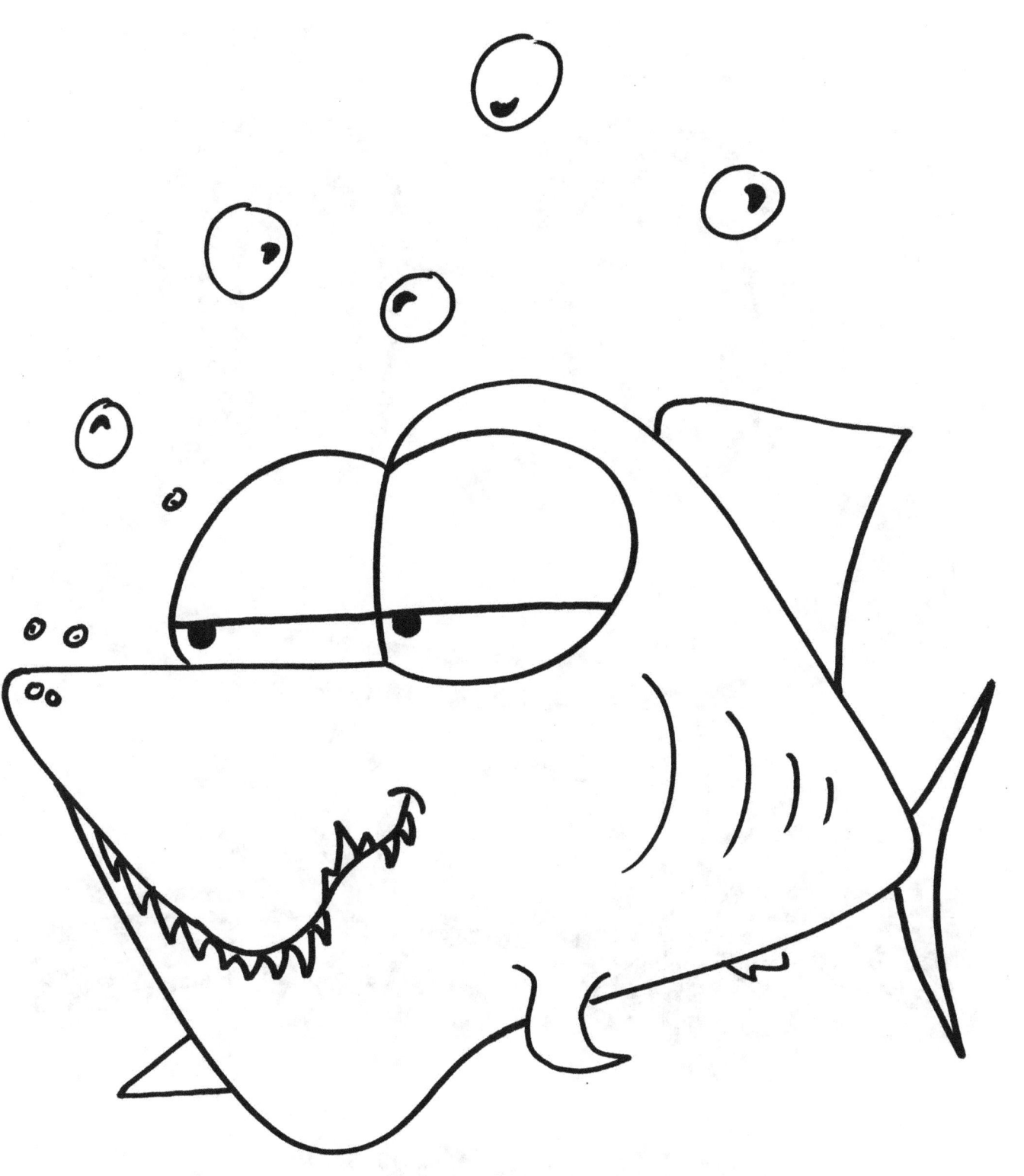

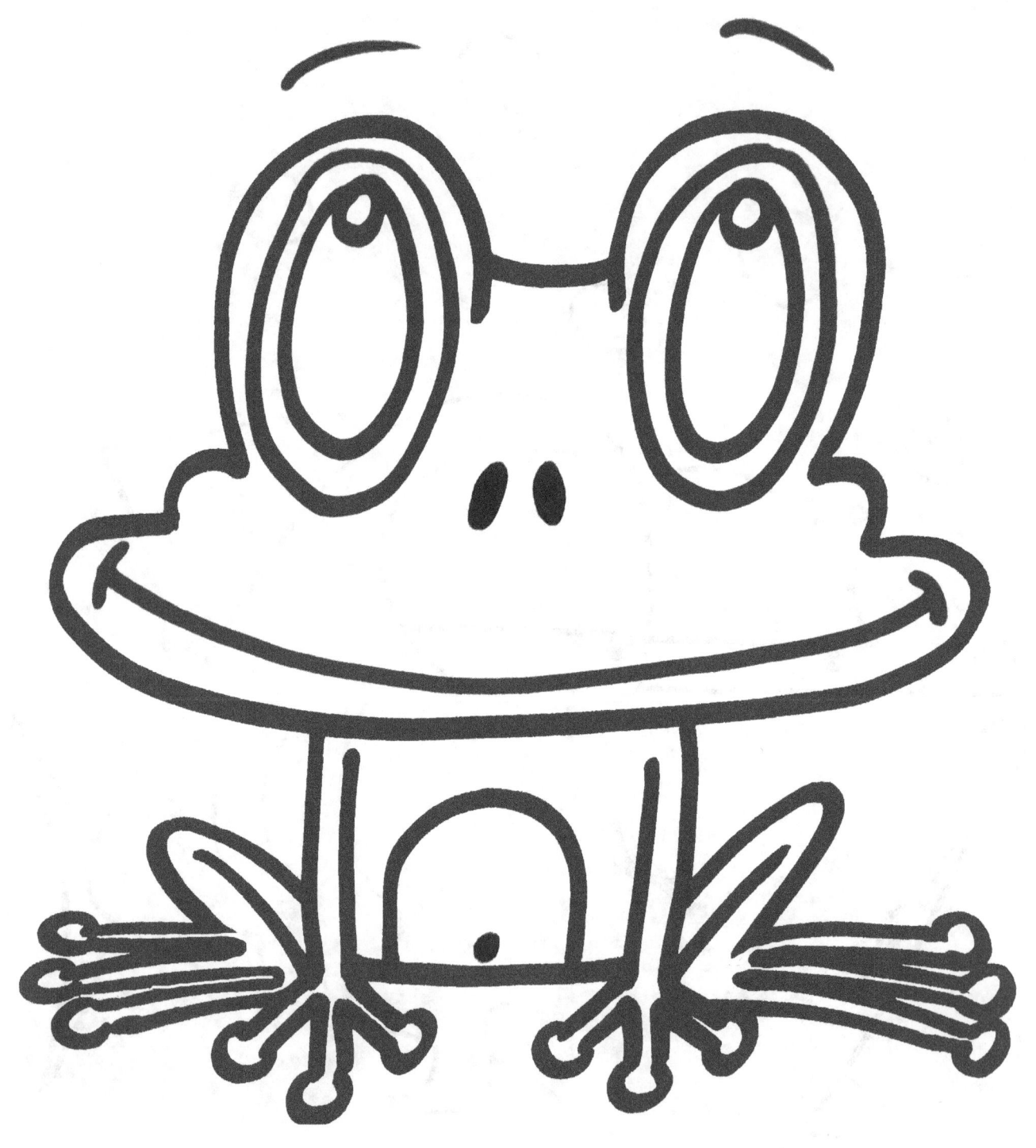

FROGS!!!

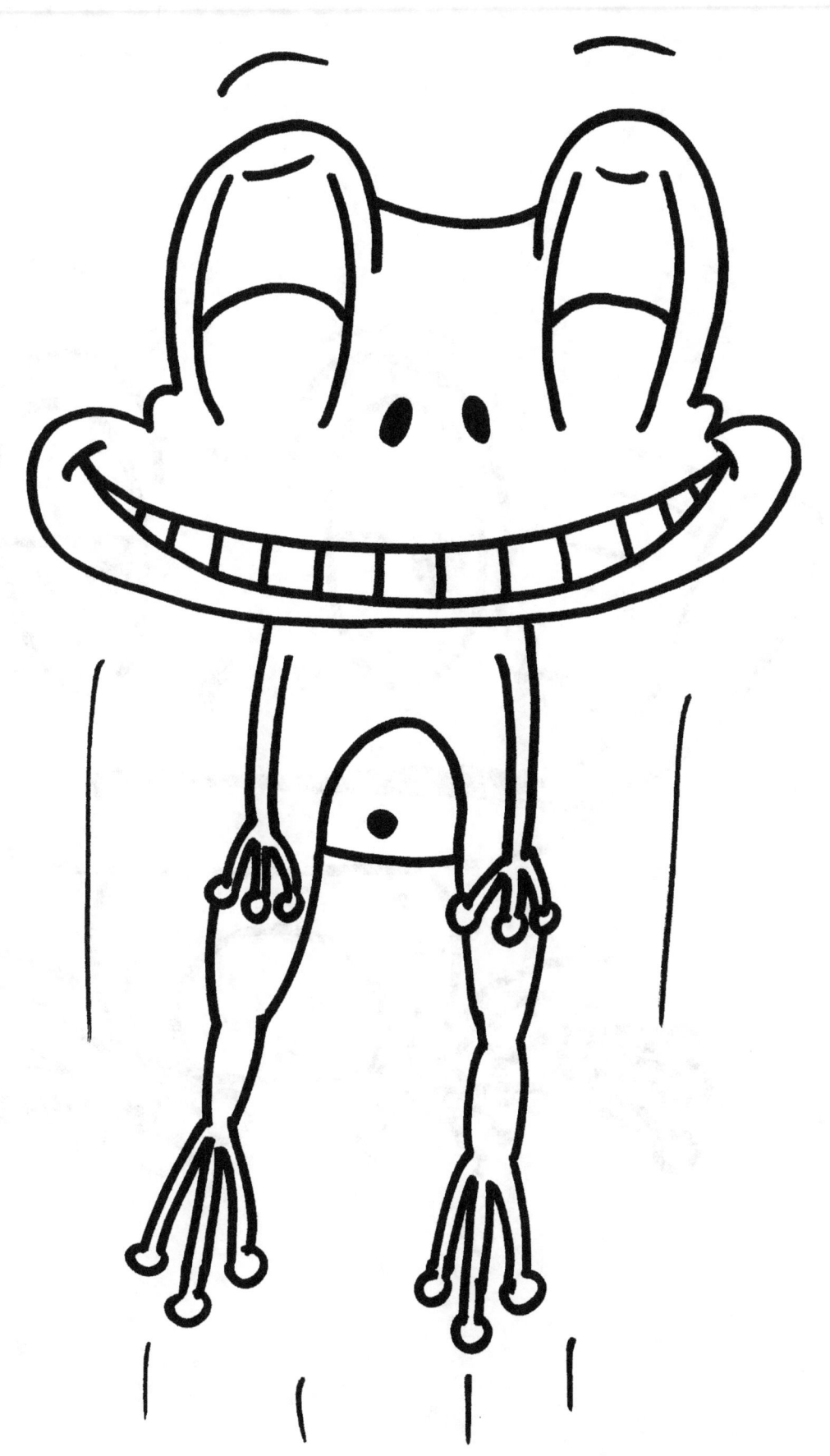

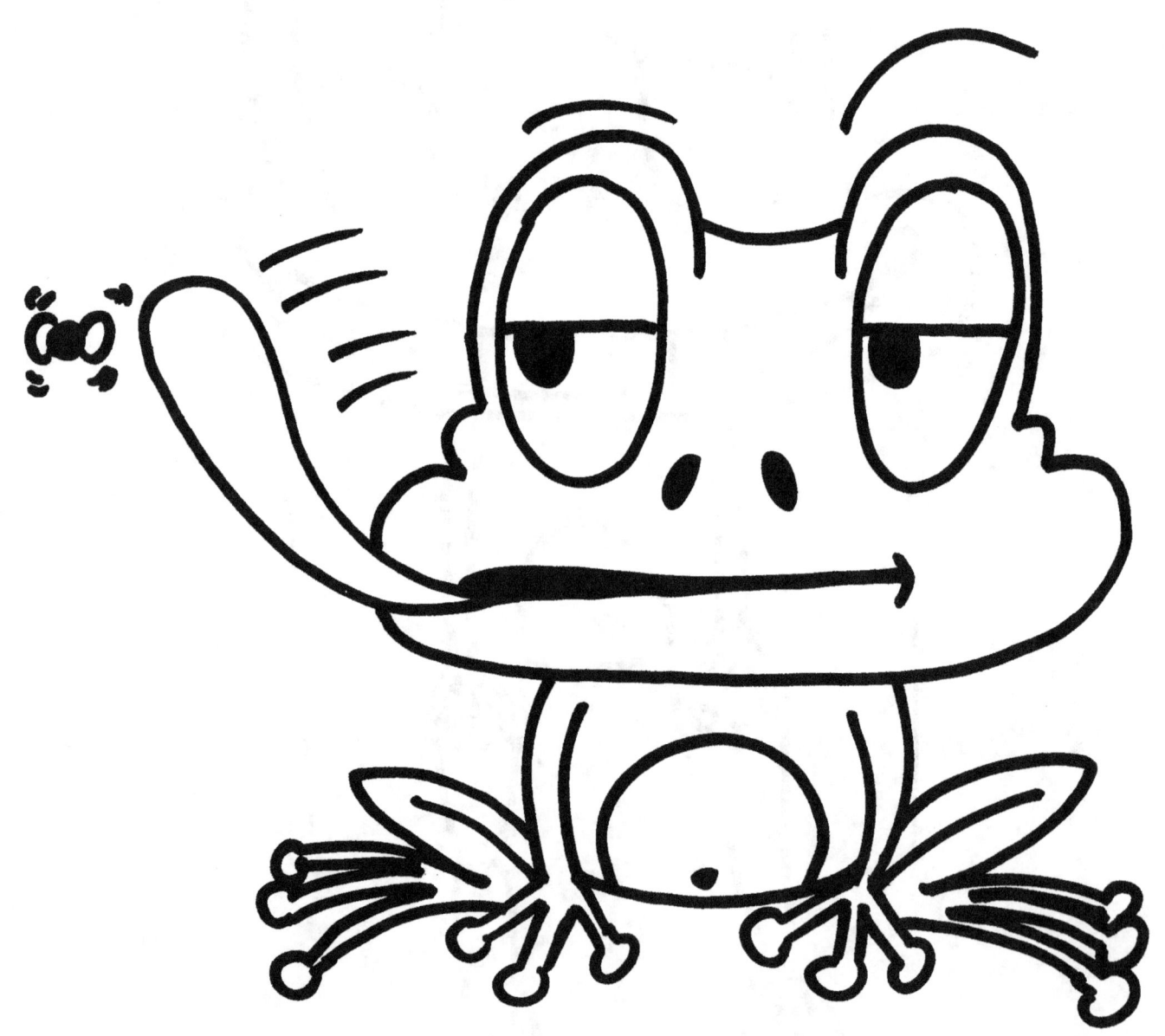

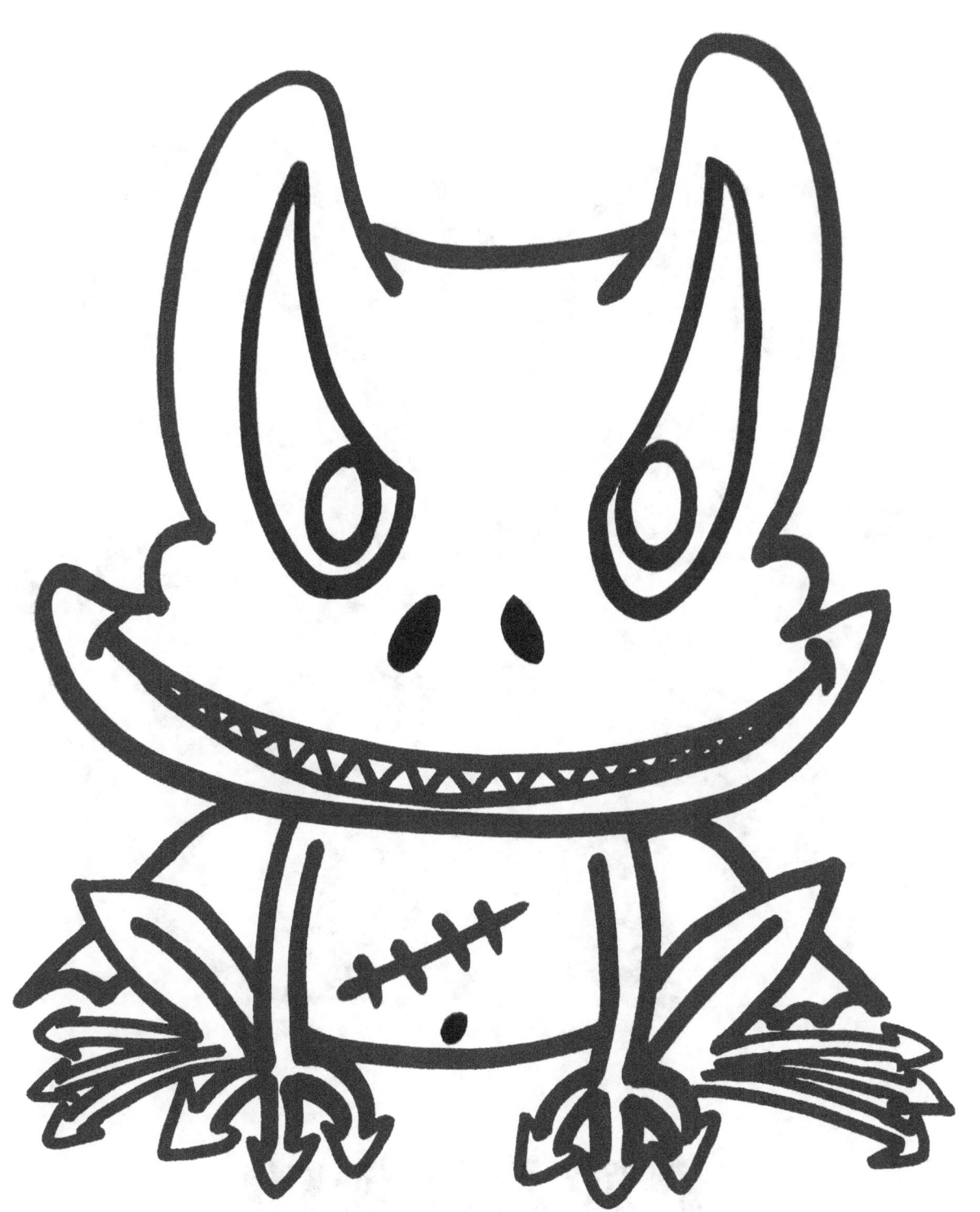

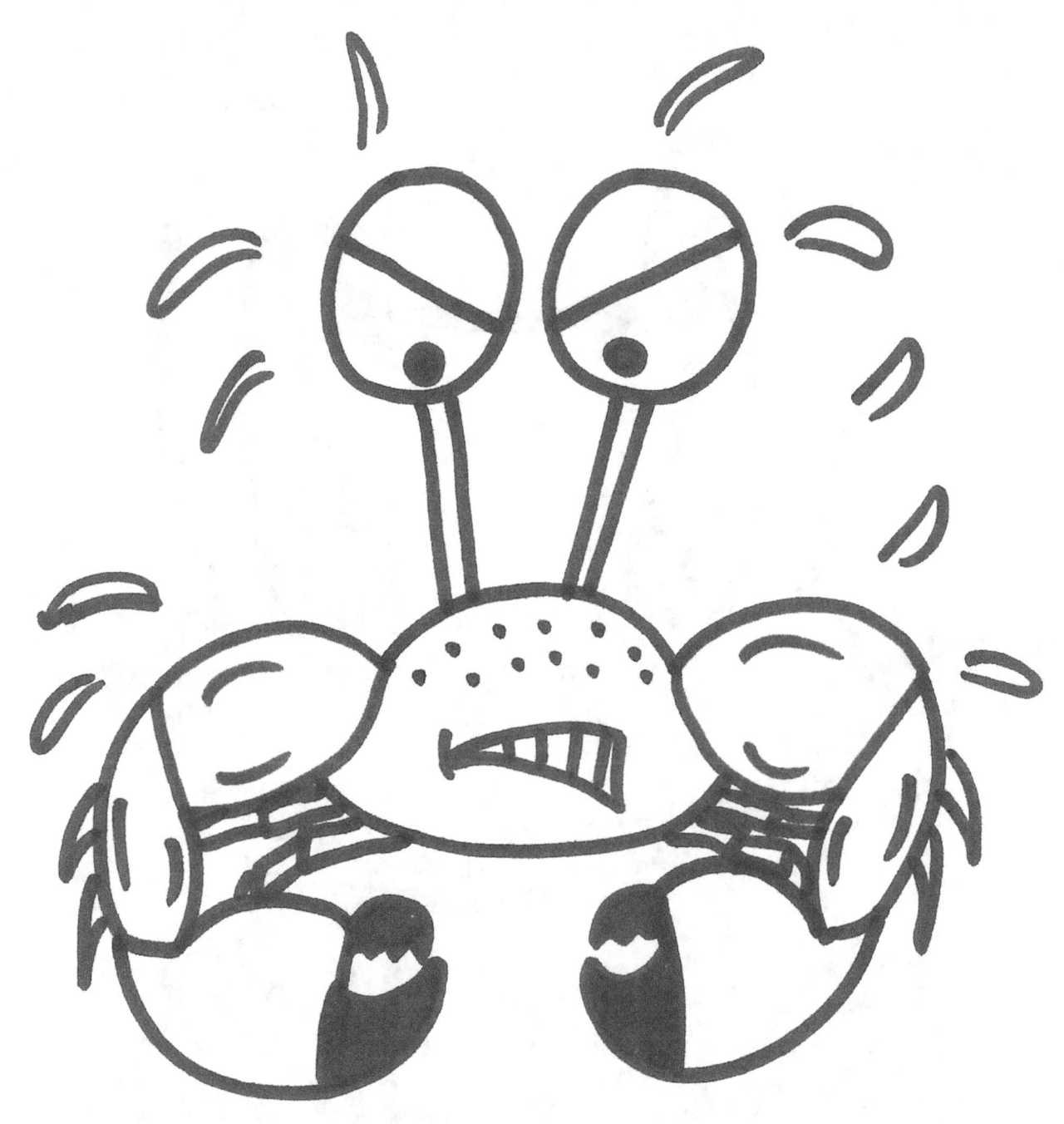

CRABS!!!

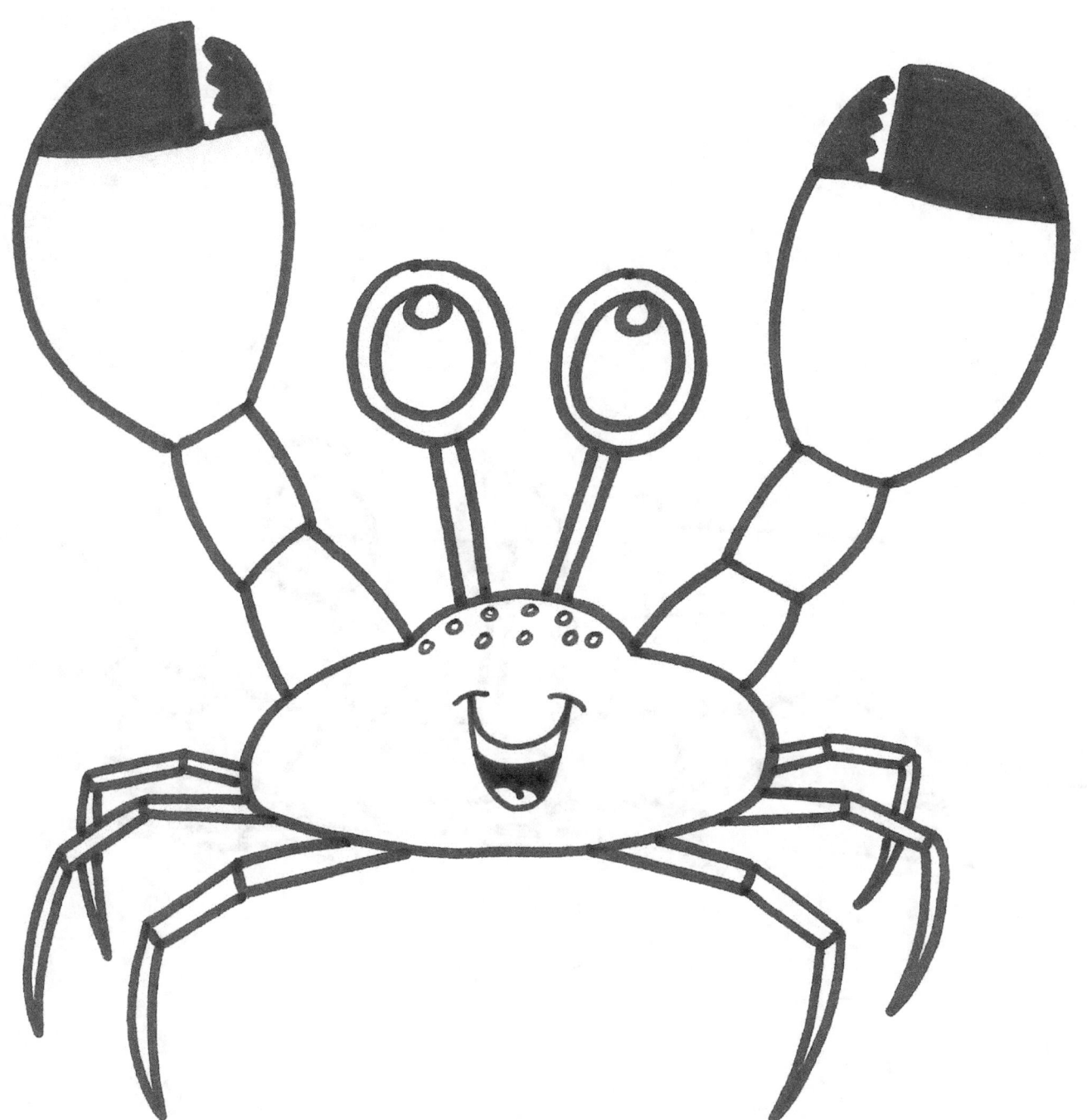

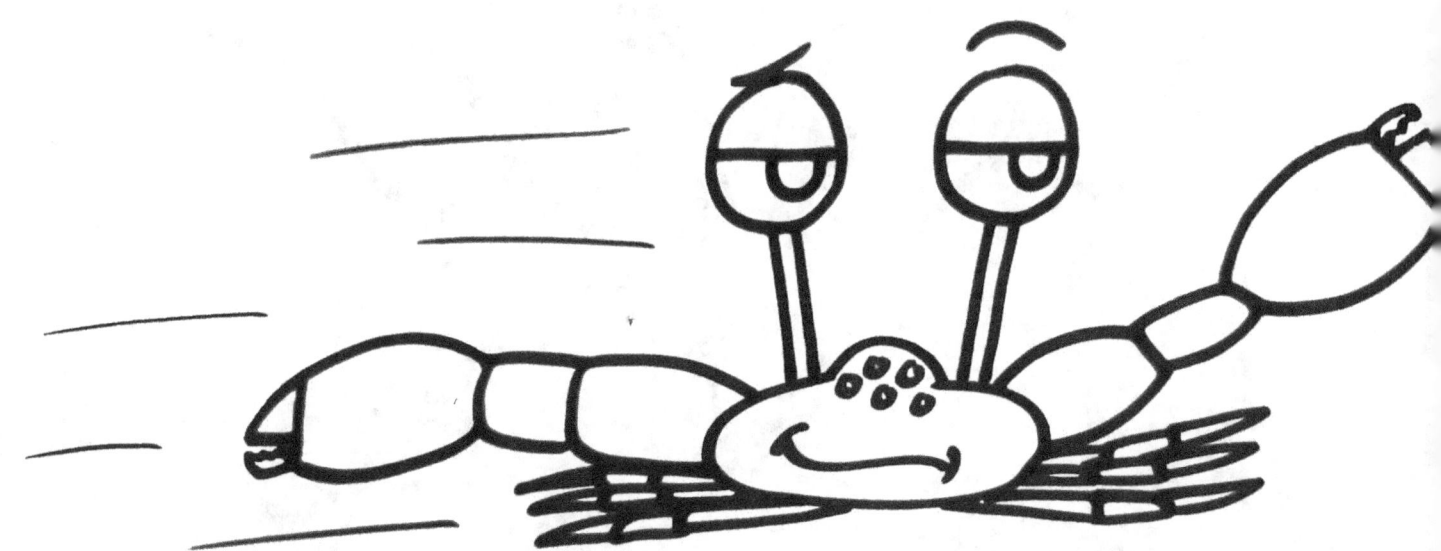

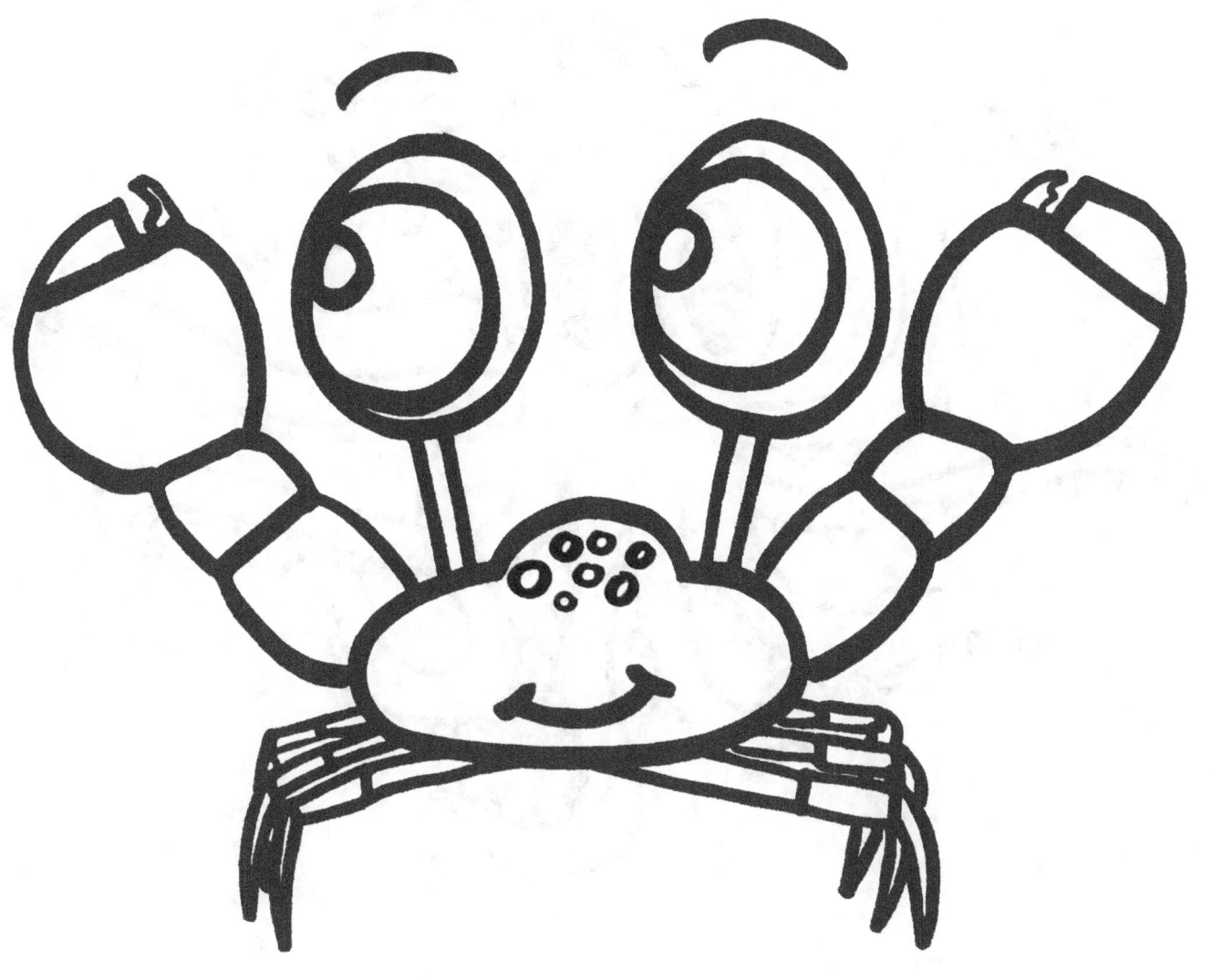

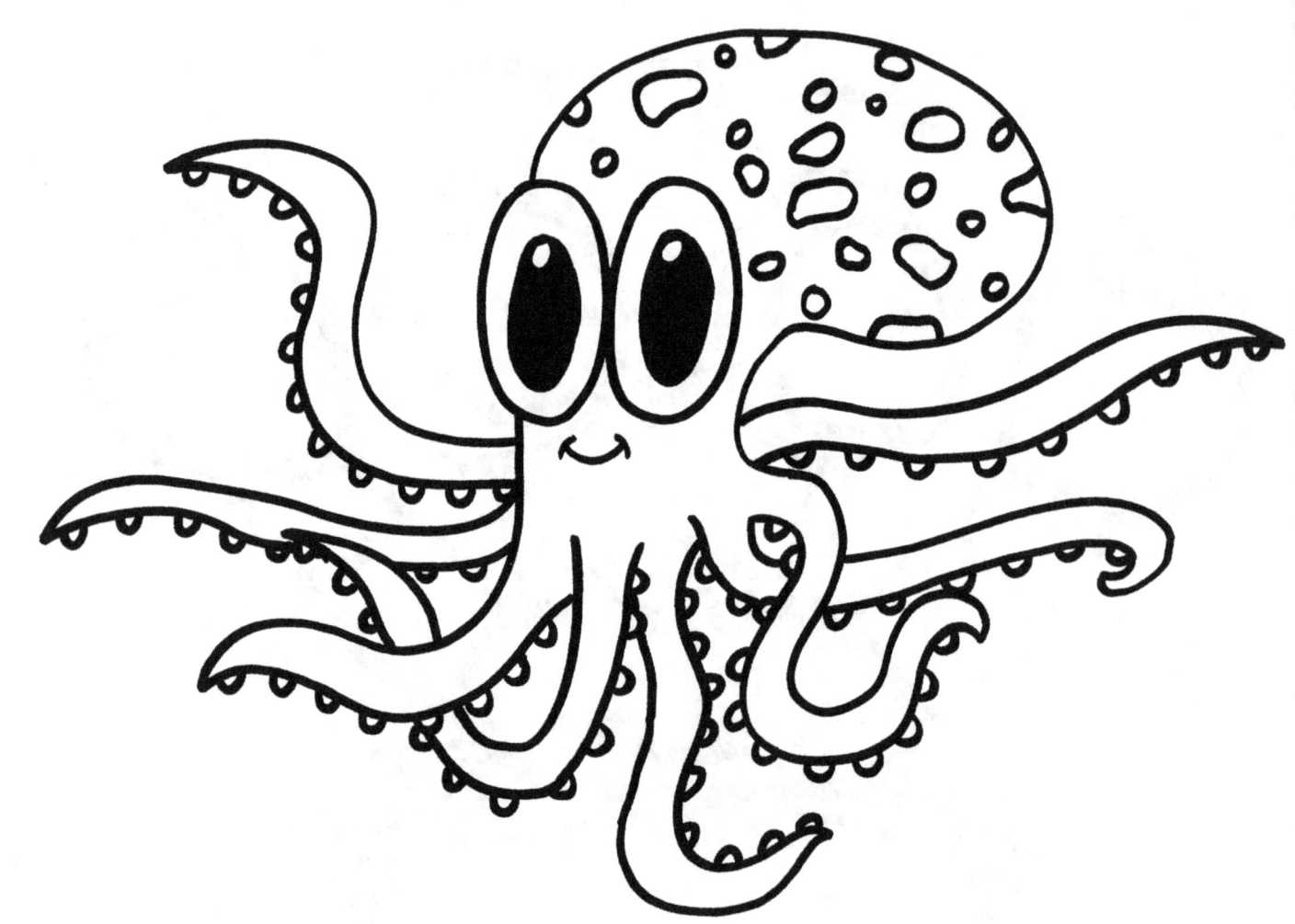

OCTOPUSES!!!

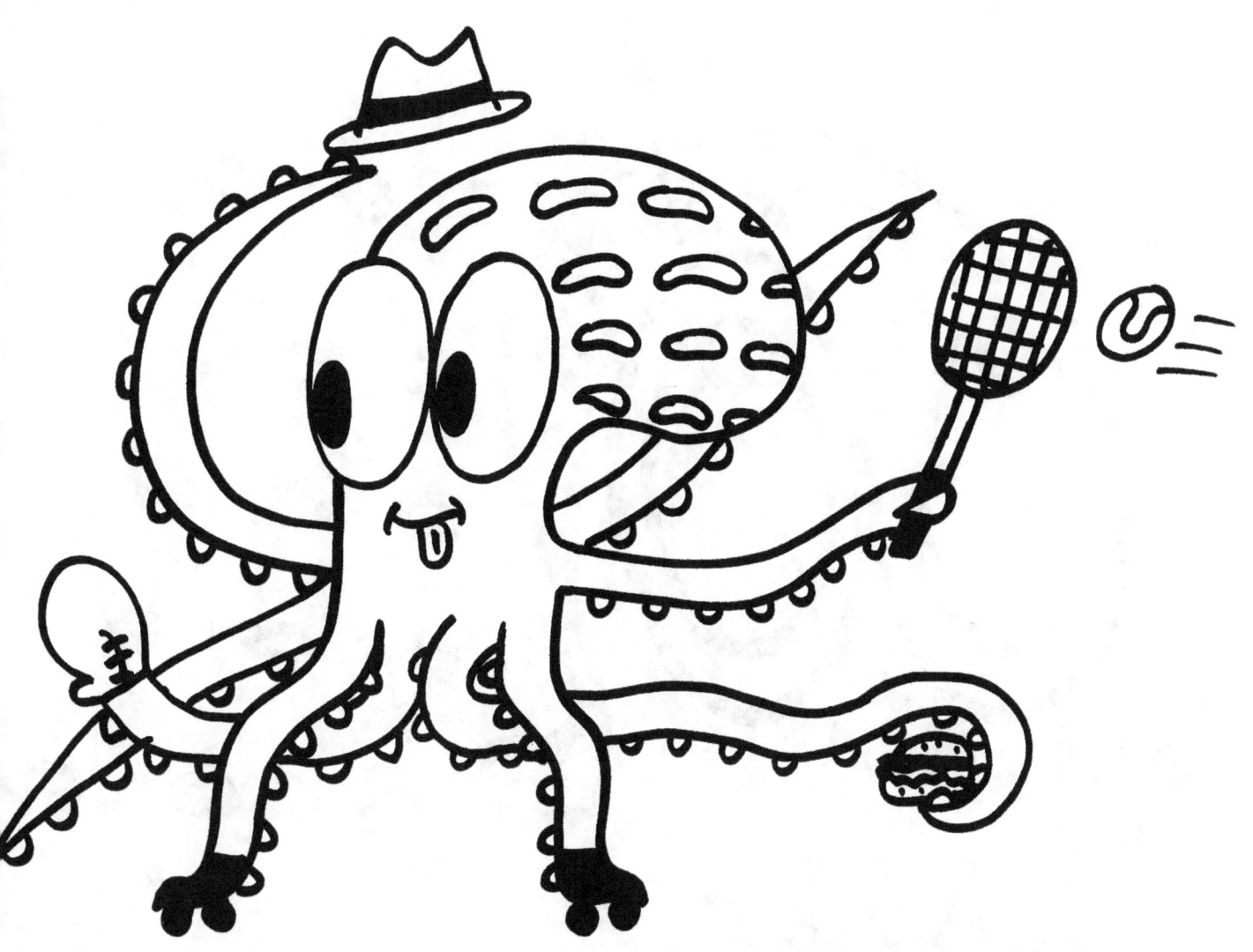

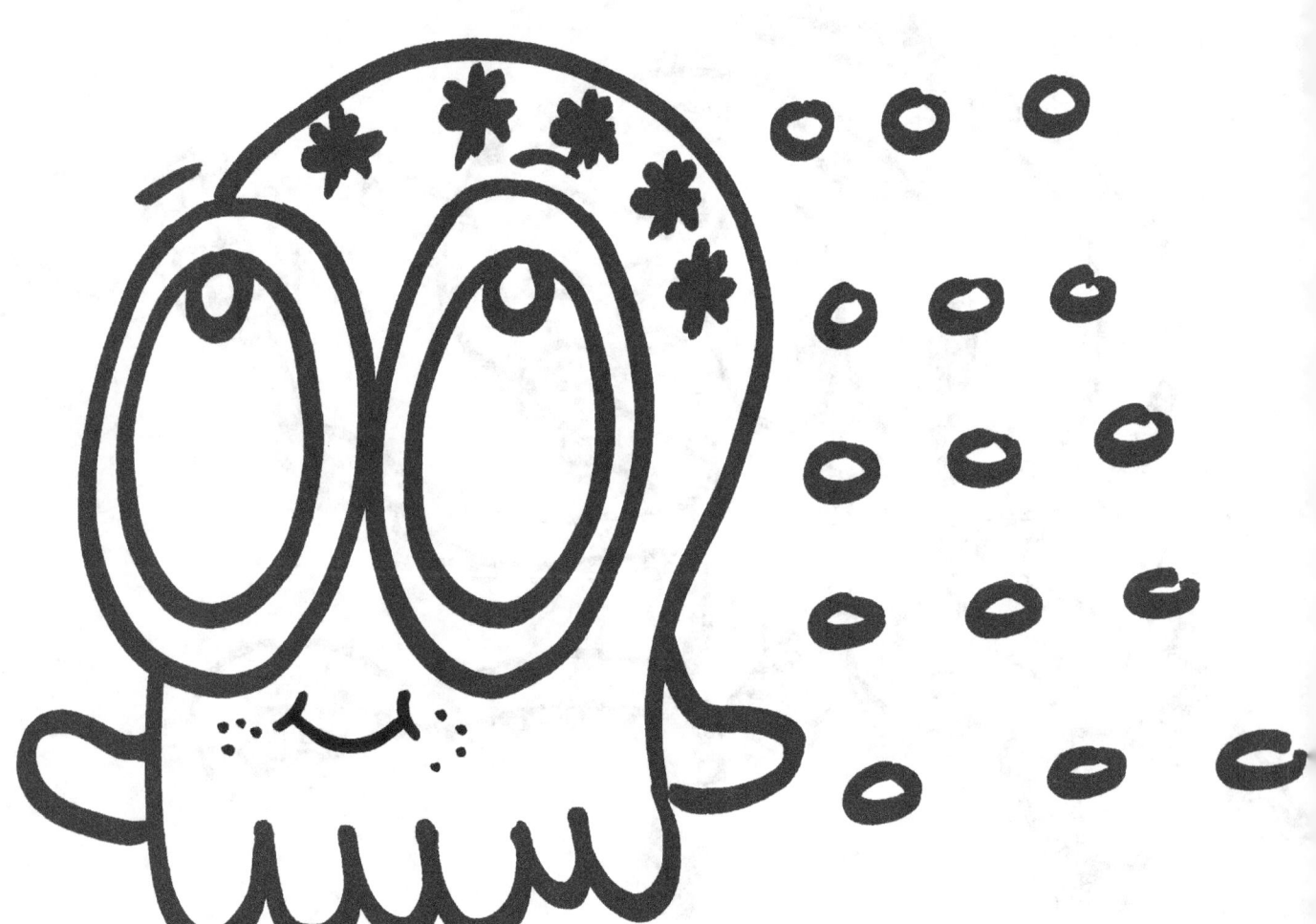

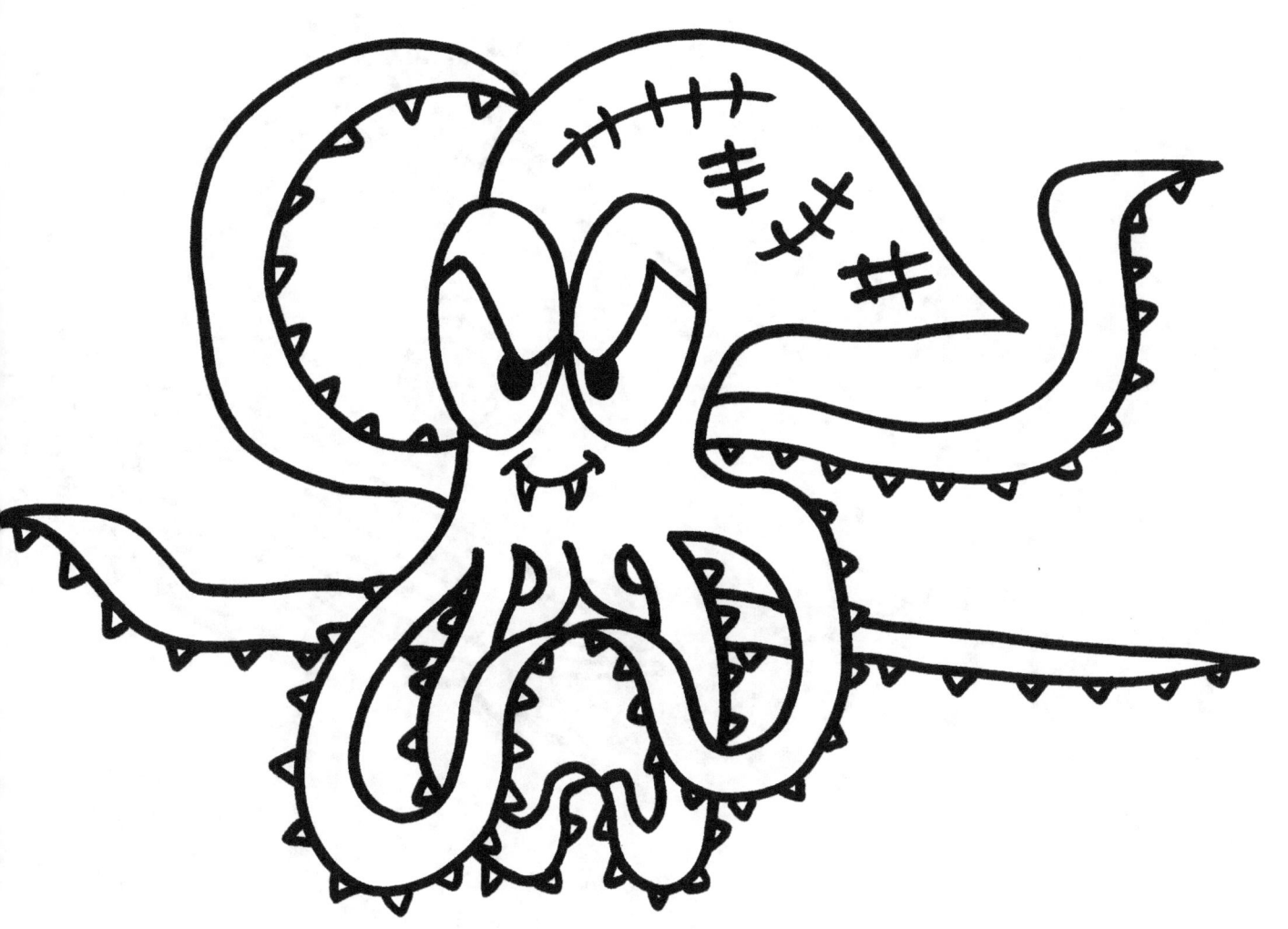

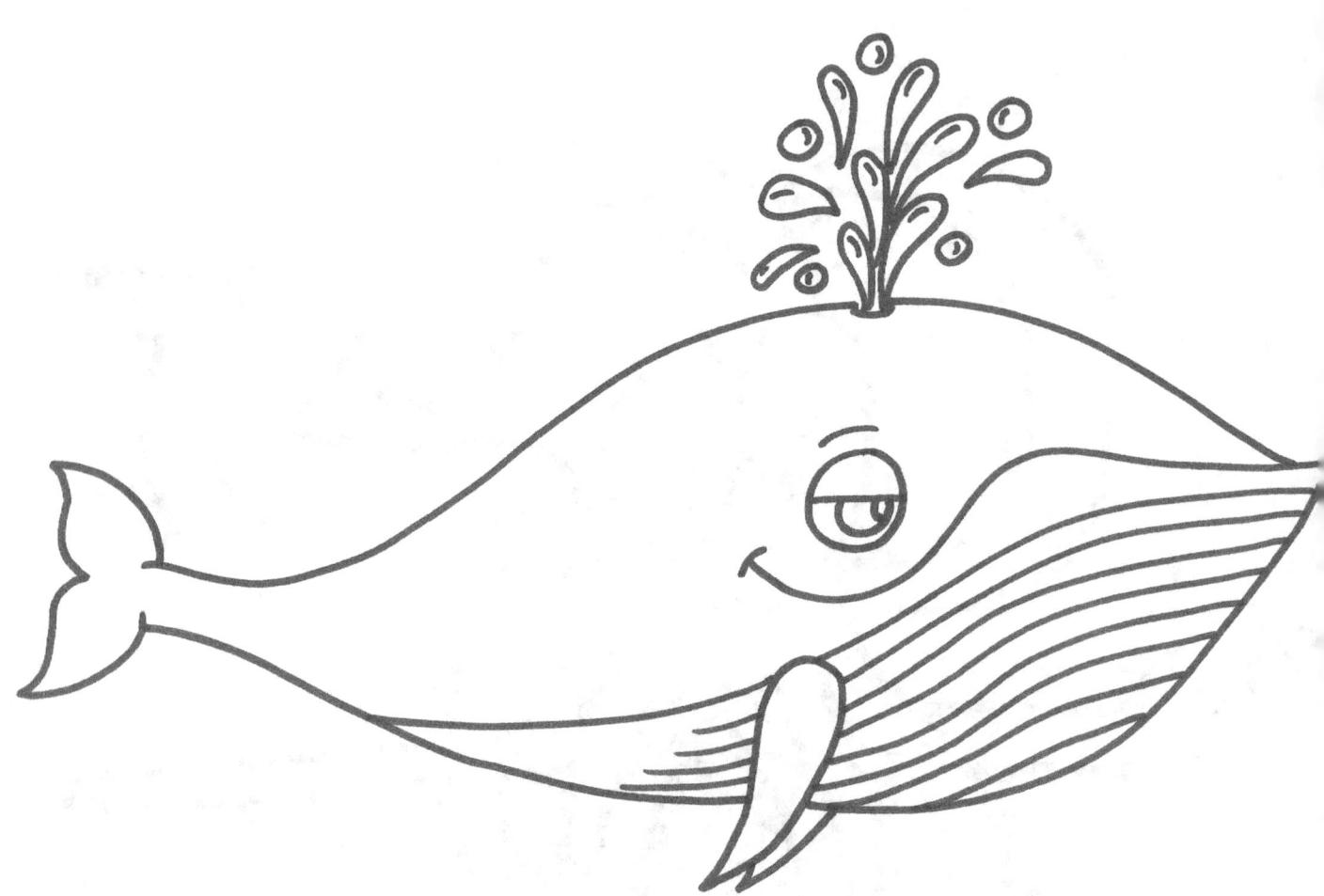

WHALES!!!

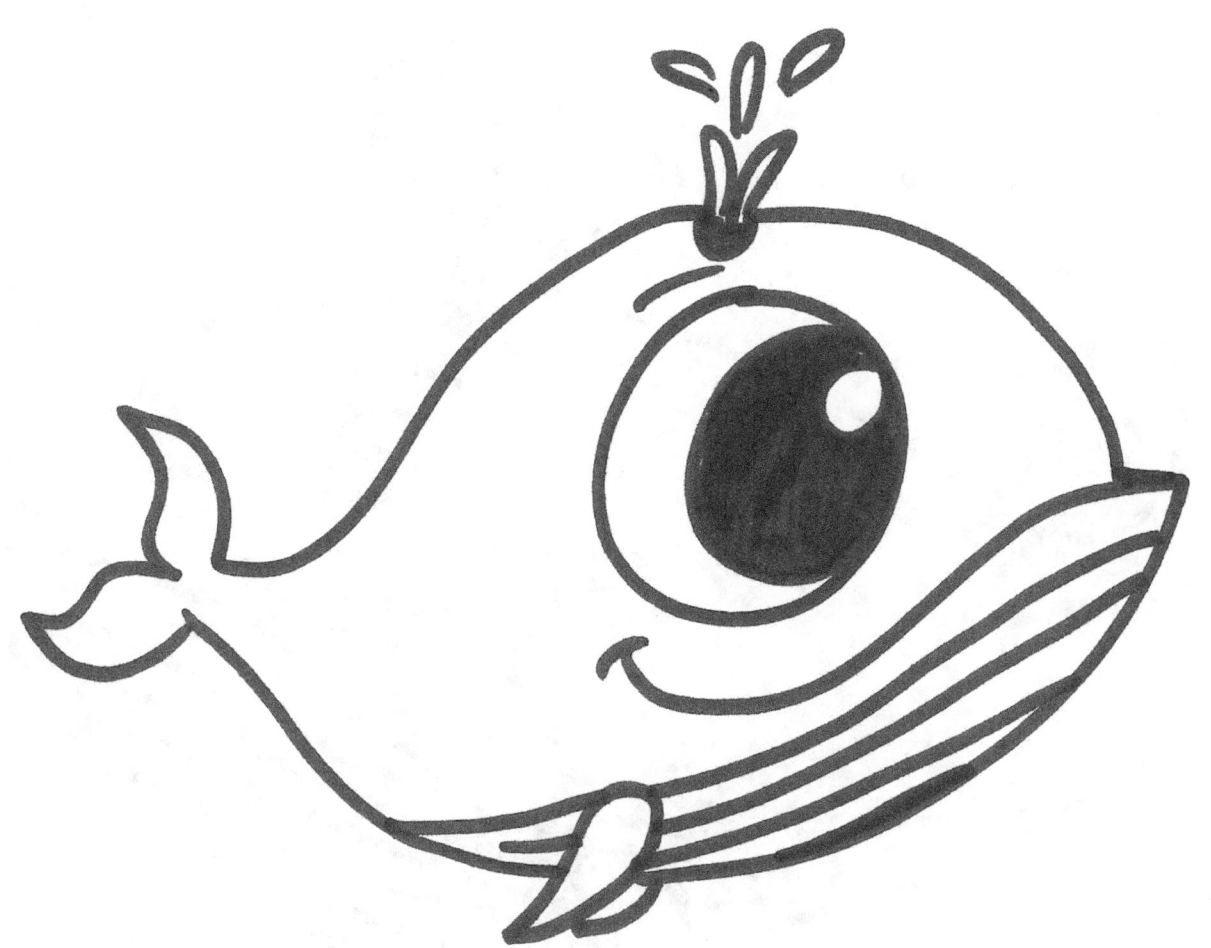

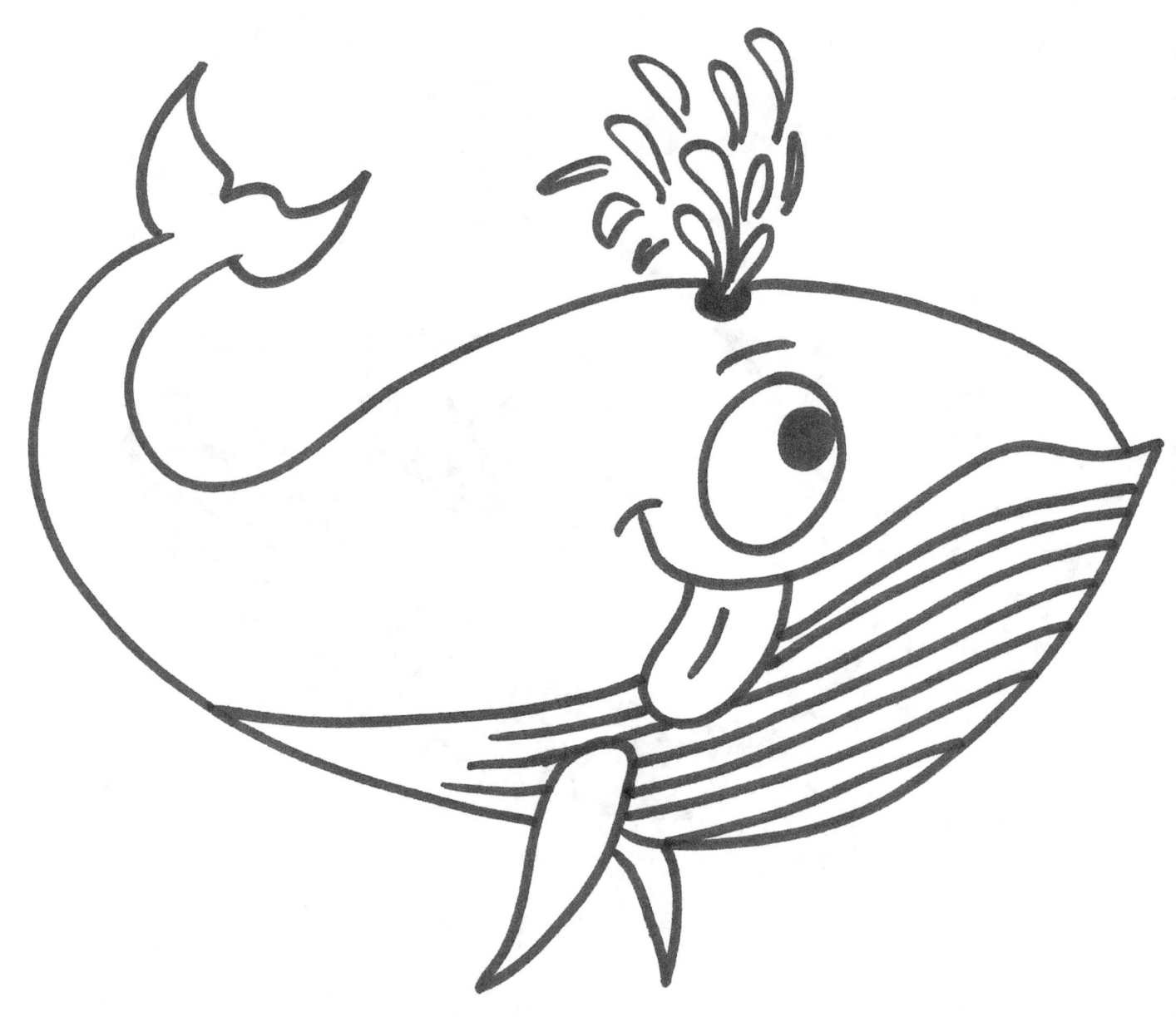

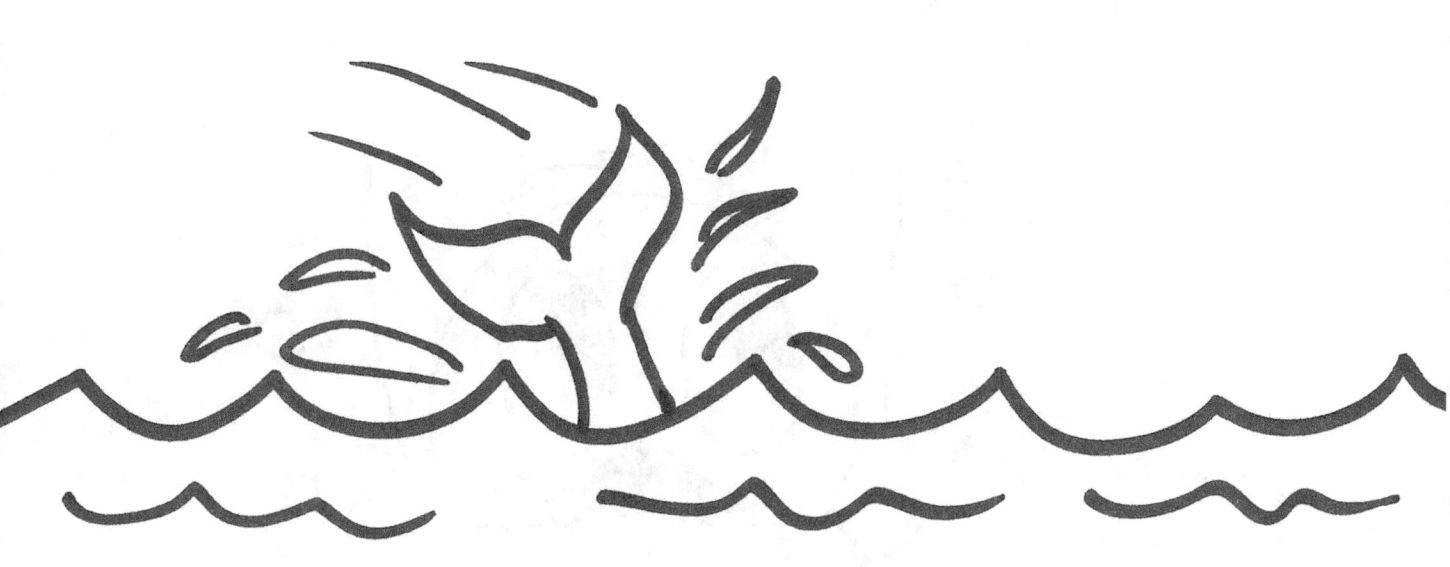

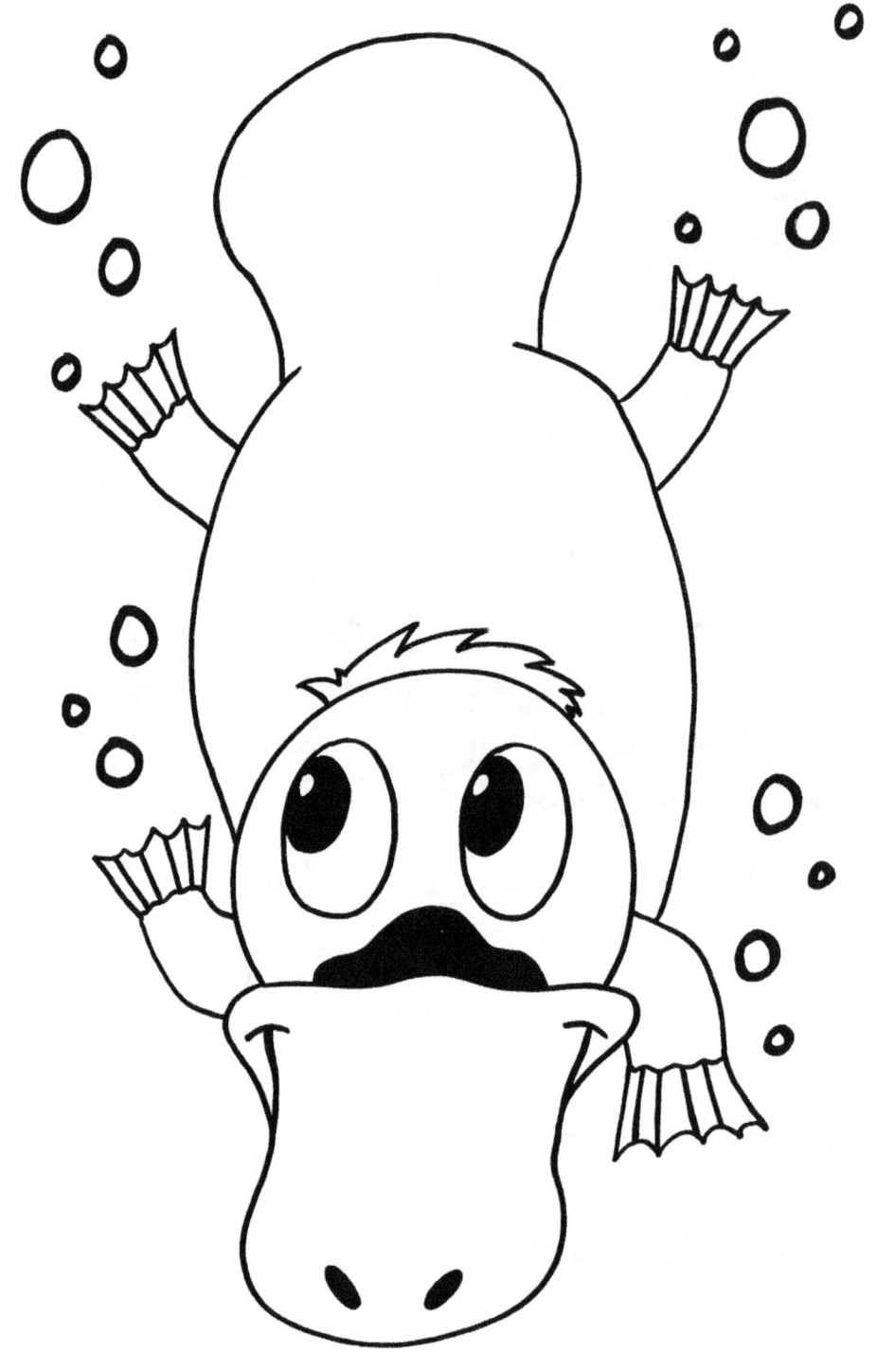

PLATYPUSES!!!

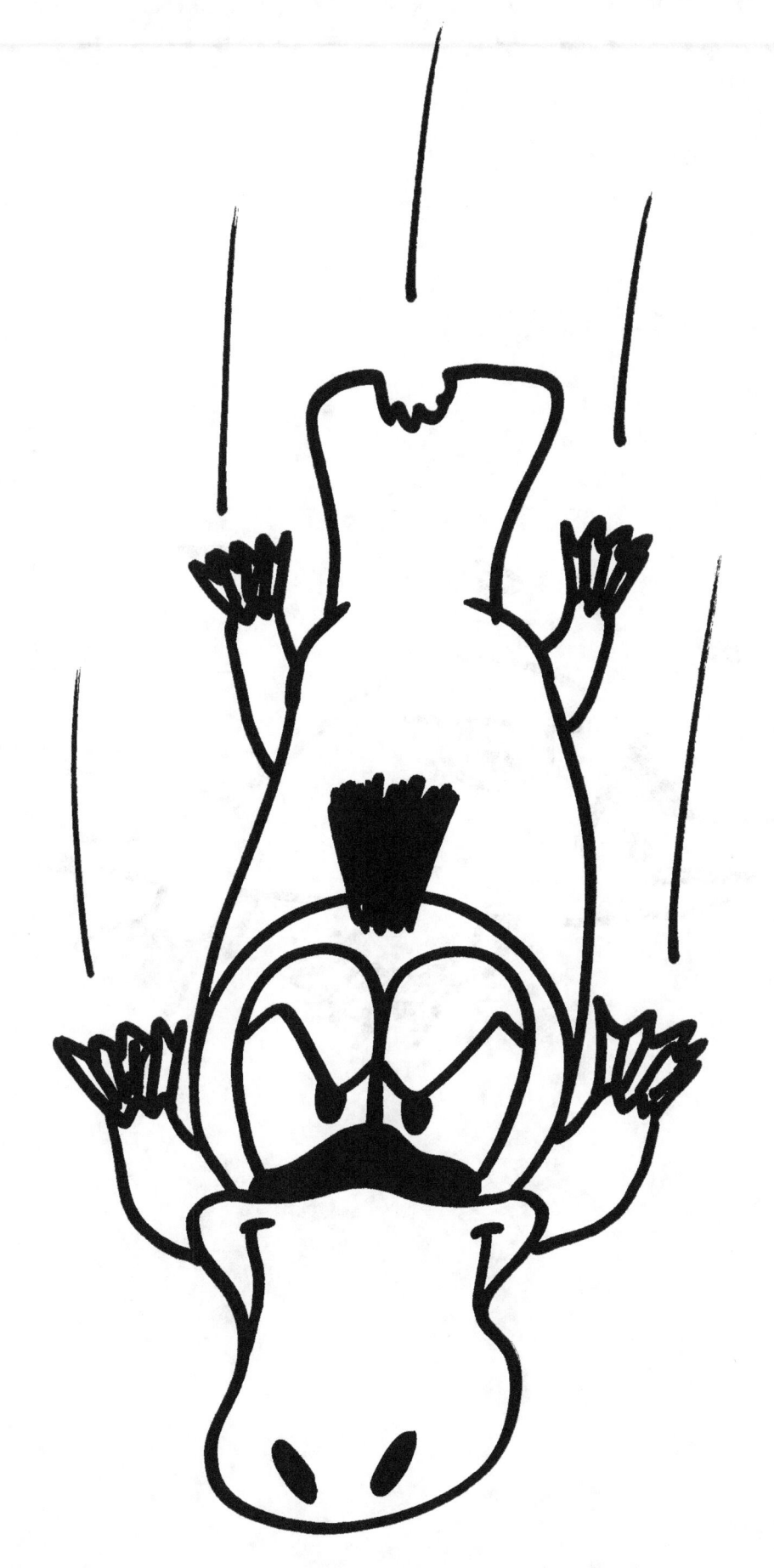

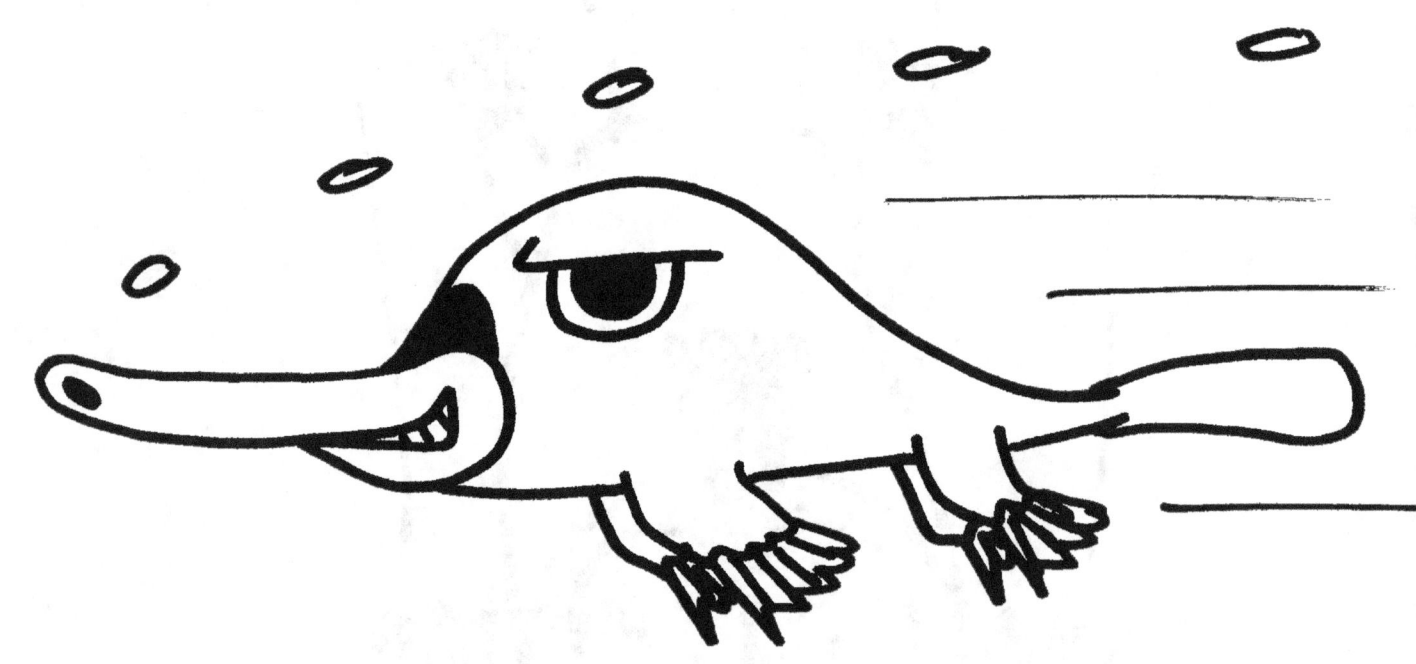

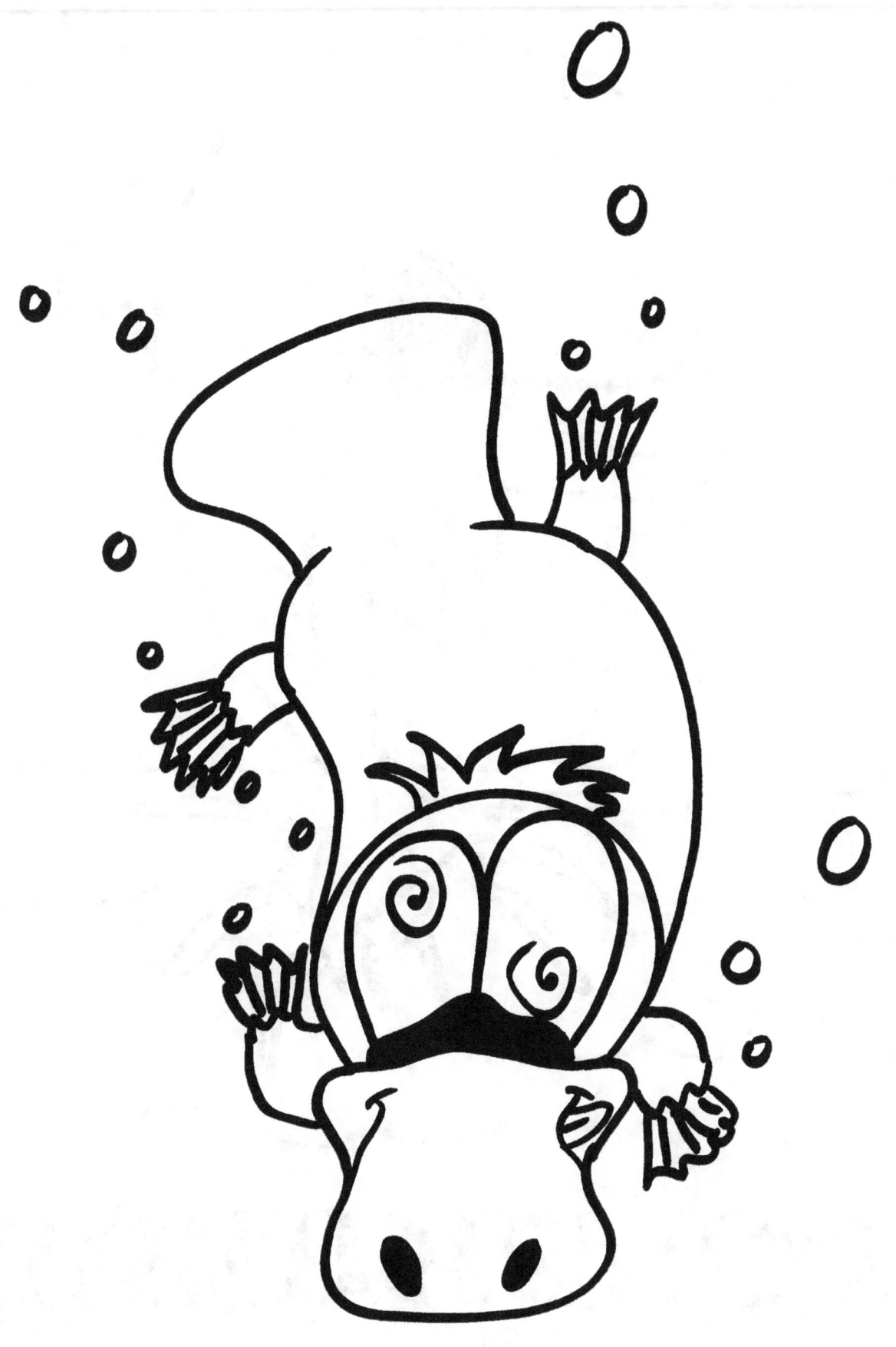

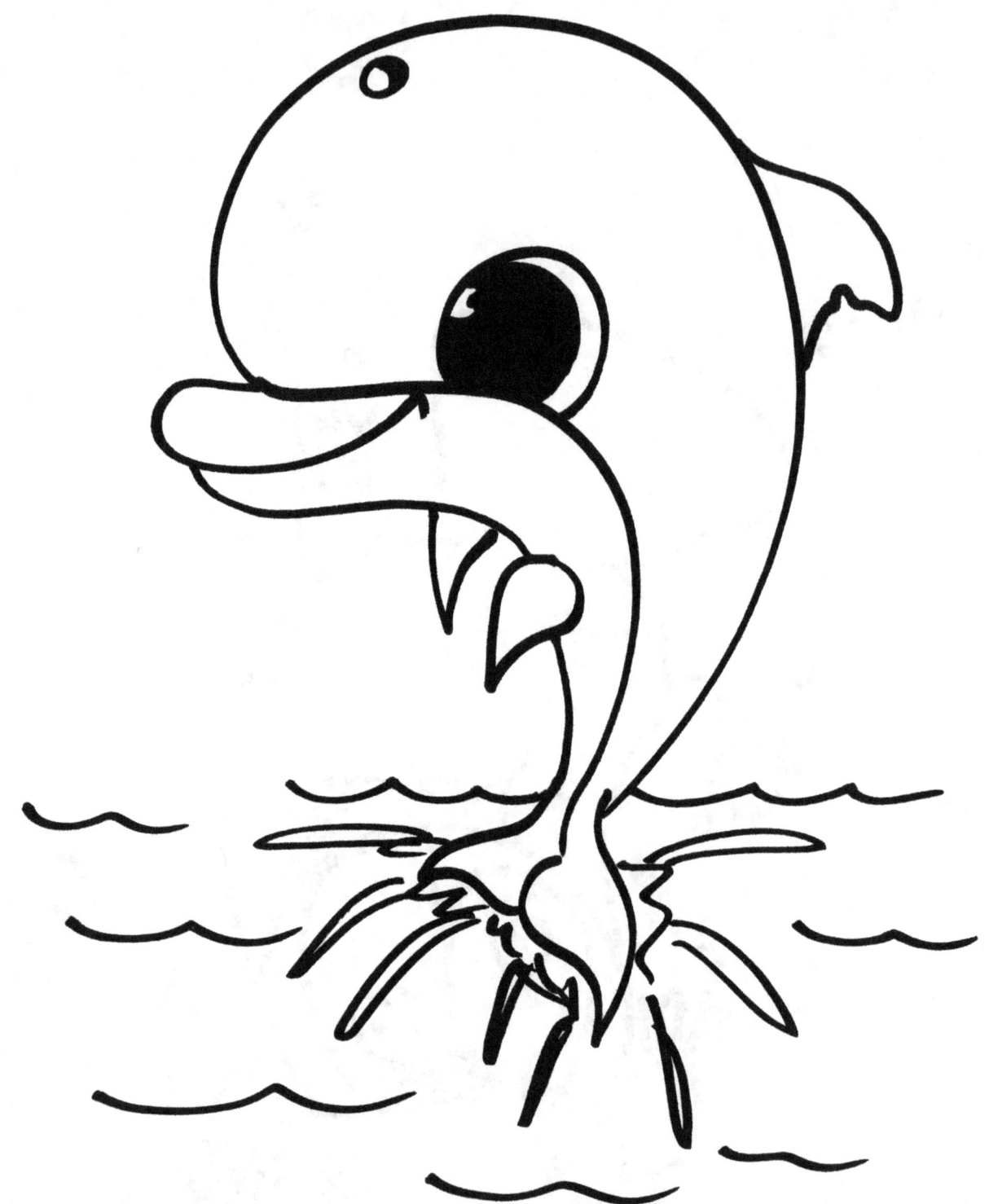

DOLPHINS!!!

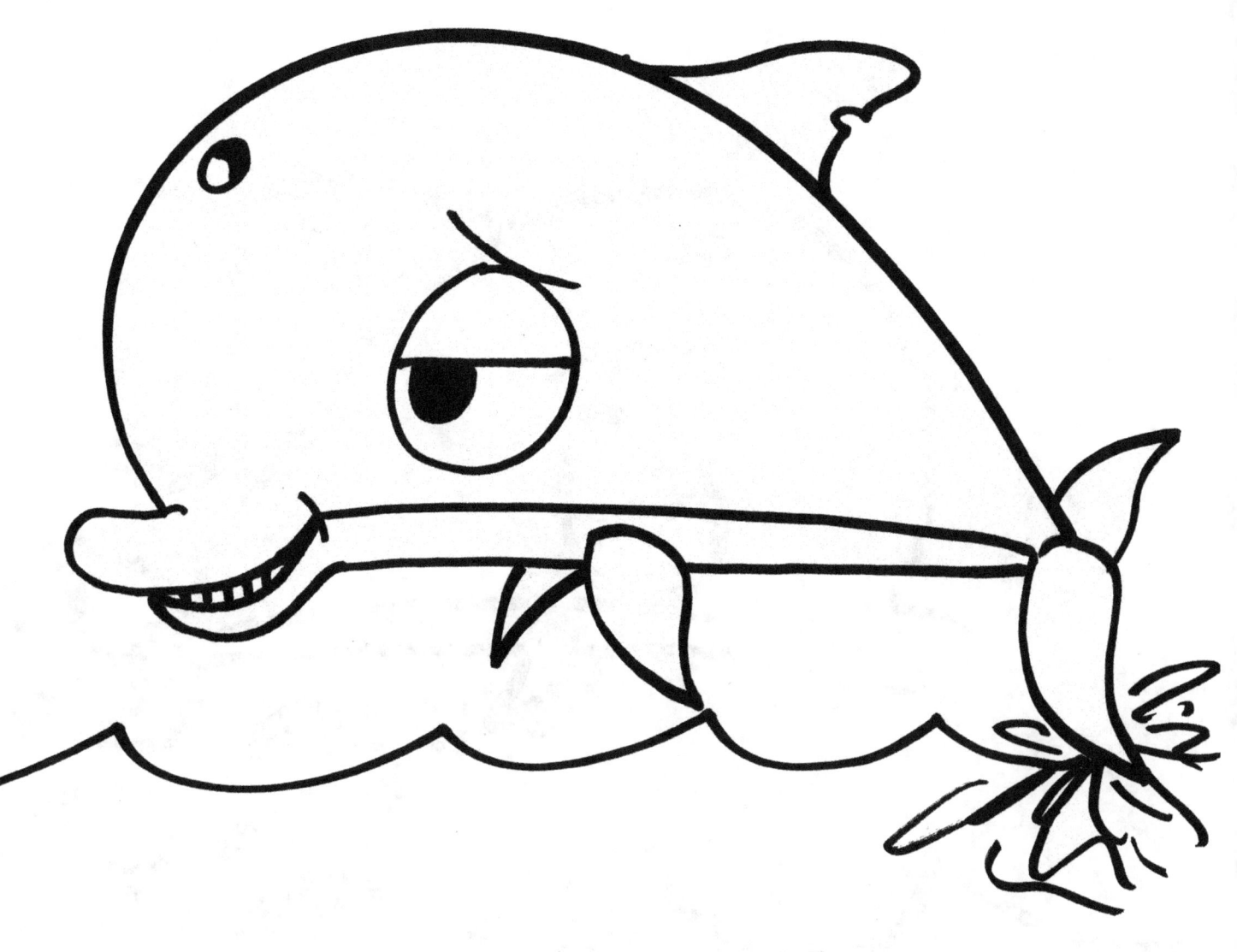

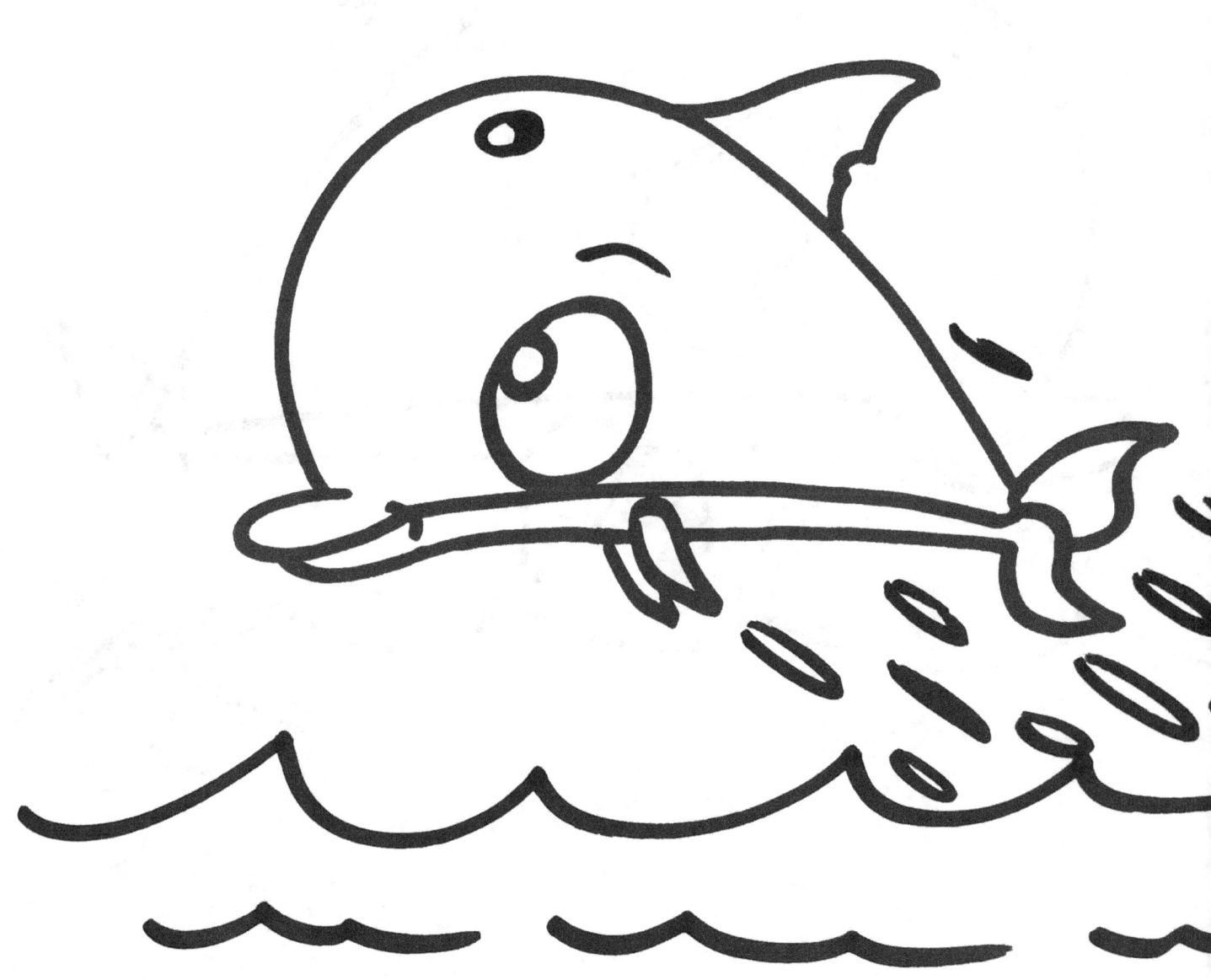

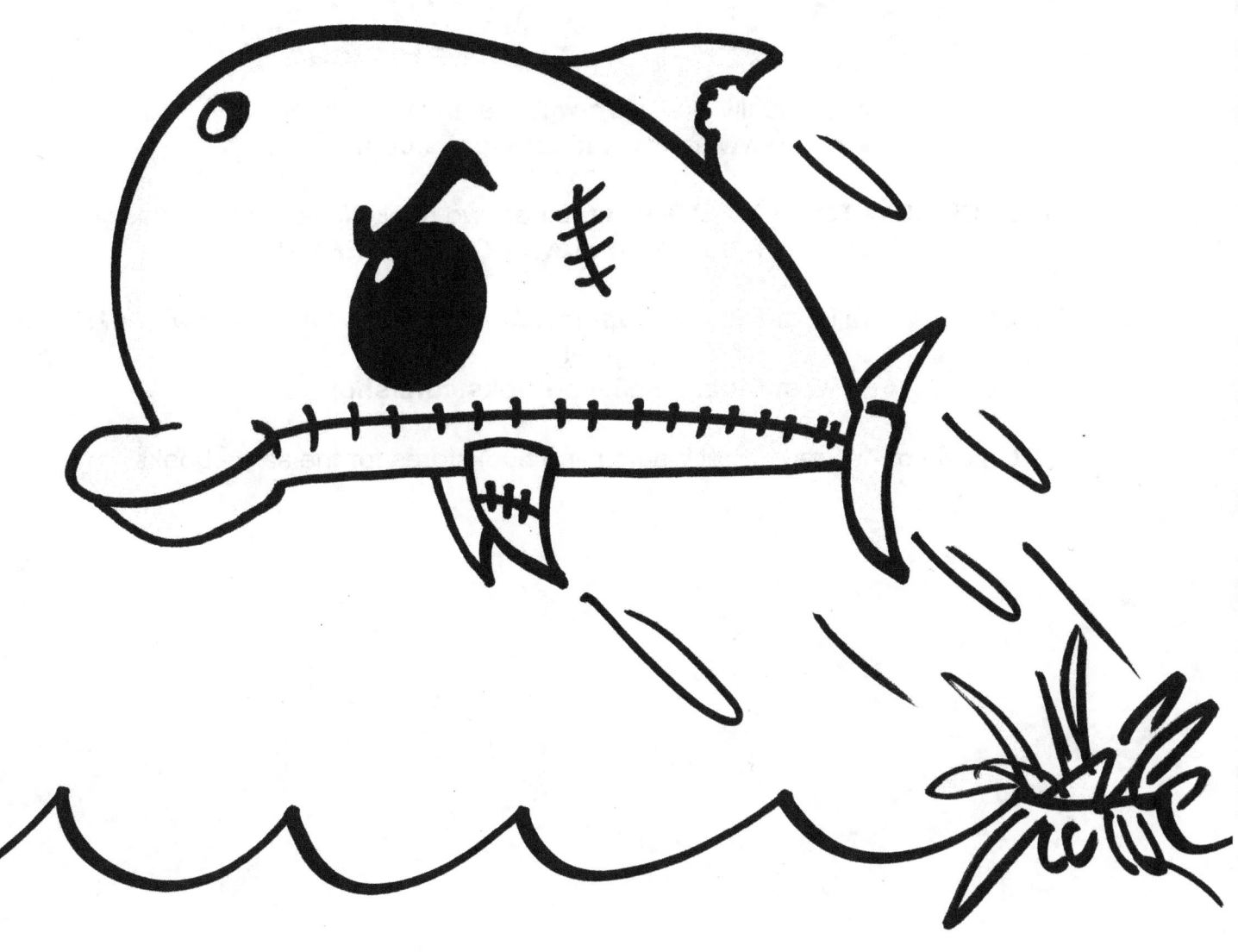

AWESOME COLOURING!

OR COLORING IF YOU ARE IN AMERICA!

If you'd actually like to *draw* these animals, check out
www.adam-wallace-books.com

The **FREE HOW TO DRAW BOOKS** tab has two books filled with animals you
can **learn how to to draw!** *FOR FREEEEE!!!*

If you're in Australia you can ***buy other Adam Wallace How to Draw books***
at
www.adam-wallace-books.com/shop

Outside of Australia, check out online bookstores for the same books!